The Potter's House

*Dr Antoasm,
Thank you
for your
Blessing.*

The Potter's House
Making of Great Persons

Samuel T. Lartey

Another Quality Book Published By:
LEGACY BOOK PUBLISHING
1883 Lee Road, Winter Park, FL 32789
www.LegacyBookPublishing.com

Unless otherwise indicated, all scripture quotations in this volume are from the New American Standard Bible (NASB) Copyright © 1960, 1962, 1963, 1968, 1971, 1972, 1973, 1975, 1977, 1995 by The Lockman Foundation

> To order additional copies of this book go to:
> **www.ThePottersHouseBook.com**
> or
> **www.LegacyBookPublishing.com**

Published by:
LEGACY Book Publishing
1883 Lee Road
Winter Park, Florida 32789
www.LegacyBookPublishing.com

Copyright ©2010 by Samuel T. Lartey
ISBN 978-1-934449-75-2
Cover Design by Gabriel H. Vaughn
Pencil Illustrations by Summer Clancy

Printed in United States of America

All rights reserved. Written permission must be secured from the publisher to use or reproduce any part of this book, except for brief critical reviews or articles.

Dedication

I dedicate this book to my mother Ms. Rosina Kuwordor. You will never know the impact and the difference you have made in my life, for single-handedly raising a family of six. Thank you for your unfailing love, care and support. Thank you a million times. I love you mum — from a grateful son.

Table of Contents

Dedication
Table of Contents 7
Foreword 9
Acknowledgements 11
Introduction 13

Section One, A Vessel of Honor

1. God the Master Potter....................... 17
2. Potters as Fathers 27
3. The Potter's Three D's 41

Section Two, 7 stages of Development

1. Breaking Period 65
2. Separation/Elimination Period 71
3. Oneness 74
4. Canvas or Upper Room Experience..... 78
5. Potter's Wheel Experience 82
6. Shelving, Cabinet or Waiting Period ... 100
7. The Furnace Fire Experience 119
Conclusion 125
A Prayer of Salvation & Confession of Faith
Bibliography
About the Author

Foreword

When I was asked to write a foreword for this book The Potter's House, I did not hesitate at all. Not because the author, Samuel Tete Lartey is one of my spiritual sons and one of my most dedicated and reliable associate pastors in the ministry to whom I regularly assign important ministerial responsibilities, but because of his remarkable passion and dedication to the things of God and his readiness to seek the direction of the Lord in all that he does.

Samuel Lartey was in his teens when I first met him at a Holy Fire Crusade in Tarkoradi in the Western Region of Ghana, West Africa in February 1990. He came forward during the anointing service to receive an impartation and since then I have personally witnessed his monumental flow and growth in ministry work. God made it possible for him to join me in the UK in 2001 as he pursued his university career in Management and International Relations.

His humility and faithfulness is a remarkable testimony of how God chooses and uses the foolish things of this earth to confound the wise. This is clearly reflected in the manuscript in the book *The Potter's House*, a book that exhibits the character and simplicity of the writer. This book is certainly a must read for believers and non-believers alike.

Samuel has documented basic truths about the handiwork of God and how through all the changing scenes of life, God can mold us into his perfect will.

The experiences of Pastor Samuel Lartey and what he has been able to achieve as a young preacher is also another testimony of what God can do in the life of an individual who is faithful and honest to his calling.

I fully endorse *The Potter's House* and recommend same to all Christians and Non-Christians as well as those who still doubt the power of the Gospel.

DR. LAWRENCE TETTEH
President/Founder
Worldwide Miracle Outreach

Acknowledgements

I want to say a big thank you to my wife Maud for her support and being a source of encouragement. My greatest appreciation goes to Dr. Lawrence Tetteh as an inspirational mentor and my pastor, Bishop Reginald Ofori-Twumasi and Apostle Solomon Yamoah for the solid foundation they laid for me to build on and the impact of revelation they made in my life.

Further, many thanks go to Dr. Koku Adomdza for unearthing the gift of writing in me and also for supervising this work. I thank him for the pressures and timescales which have really yielded fruits beyond measure. I want to say a very big thank you to my one and only big brother, the great apostle Charles Offei Lartey and my sisters; I am so proud of you. To all my friends at End-time Youth fellowship, the NEC and Hofirm, not forgetting Ms. Elaine Hope Palmer for proofreading and working alongside Dr. Koku and Maud. Many thanks to Gabriel Vaughn of Legacy Book Publishing for a great work done.

My in-laws, Mr. and Mrs. Abadoo Brew, for their unfailing love and their great support. Thank you Rev. Dr. Mensa Otabil, the Chancellor of Central University, for awarding me with an academic scholarship from 1992 to 1994. Mrs. Barbara Tetteh and Mr. Yeboah Dacosta for their great support for me and my family. Rev. Dominic Kwofie and Rev. Noble Kwagie for their great counselling and advice when I first started the Journey.

I am really grateful to The Potter's House book launch planning committee at WMO Youth for an outstanding and very great work done prior to the launching of this book. Thank you Barrister Lawumi Biriyok for your support and love.

Introduction

The truth and the revelation of the potter's house: the potter, the clay and their daily relevance to man is yet to be understood by all.

> *"Arise and go down to the potter's house, and there I will announce My words to you." Then I went down to the potter's house, and there he was, making something on the wheel. But the vessel that he was making of clay was spoiled in the hand of the potter; so he remade it into another vessel, as it pleased the potter to make. Then the word of the LORD came to me saying, "Can I not, O house of Israel, deal with you as this potter does?" declares the LORD. "Behold, like the clay in the potter's hand, so are you in My hand, O house of Israel.*
> **Jeremiah 18:2-6**

I had the inspiration to write *The Potter's House* when I was writing about developing gift and talent, about the need and the role of the father as a coach who can take an ordinary individual with some gift and then develop him into a highly sought after professional. I was motivated to write this book because I realized that the changing scenes of life can very much be compared to the processes that the potter uses in making a vessel. The fact that these vessels or earthen wares are used by priests, kings, queens, secretary generals, presidents etc to serve and to decorate their temples where worship is made to God is quite significant. Royal palaces and offices which receive cherished guests are made from marred clay mined from the remotest part of the country and not from the city centers. I am amazed by the fact that people who are despised and who are often treated with no regard, after an encounter with God, the master potter; he makes something beautiful from their shattered lives. Subsequently, they are sought after by the high priests, the royals and the nobles in society. They are ready to pay whatever price it would cost them to acquire these changed individuals.

> The factors associated with the definitive onset of this book are:
> - God as our potter
> - Human beings as the clay
> - God making us the vessel he intends us to be
> - God making us useful.

The key message of this book is that regardless of who you are and where you are, God can make you into the vessel of honor for His purposes, if only you will be patient and allow Him to take you through His own processes to the very end.

This book is relevant to contemporary times, because these days everyone wants to be celebrated in his or her field of endeavour. Although we all want to be great and are all looking for lasting success, only a few become successful and are achievers. Because they understand and allow themselves to follow ardently the potter's seven processes, they are unlike most of us who fail because we want instant success and are not ready to follow laid down principles.

This book:
- gives answers about why young talents fail
- explains why great missions and visions die before they are ever realized
- teaches you the seven processes everyone goes through before they can experience real lasting success and fulfill their God-given purpose on earth
- shows you why a gift without a father cannot make it.
- explains why when a gift comes out all of a sudden, it can disappear in the same way
- demonstrates that great gifts are defeated by seemingly insignificant, not-so-good attitudes.

Above all, this book is written to all who want to become super achievers of their dreams, goals and their God-given assignments in life. Furthermore, it will benefit all who greatly want to understand those processes of life and will help them to follow the processes to fulfill their dreams and purpose in life.

Chapter 1

God the Master Potter

Chapter One

GOD THE MASTER POTTER

> *"Arise and go down to the potter's house, and there I will announce My words to you." Then I went down to the potter's house, and there he was, making something on the wheel. But the vessel that he was making of clay was spoiled in the hand of the potter; so he remade it into another vessel, as it pleased the potter to make. Then the word of the LORD came to me saying, "Can I not, O house of Israel, deal with you as this potter does?" declares the LORD. "Behold, like the clay in the potter's hand, so are you in My hand, O house of Israel.*
> **Jeremiah 18:2-6**

This is an essential passage which consists of exciting revelations of God the potter and Israel or his children being the clay and how He the potter molds us into a vessel out of crushed clay.

Jeremiah 18:3 reveals how the prophet was ready to learn God's way of dealing with his people by discovering them as clay and then taking them to His house developing them and dispatching them to be a blessing to the nations of the world.

Personally, I believe it is good for everyone to visit a pottery at least once in his or her lifetime to discover the processes the potter uses to transform ordinary clay to a vessel used by men of honor. It is so interesting to witness an earthly potter molding a vessel. It is an effective way of learning how God deals with his children. That is why he said to Jeremiah, "go down to the potter's house to learn." This message from the potter's house is relevant to us in every life situation.

In Jeremiah 18:5-6 and Isaiah 64:8 God is the Potter and human beings are the clay. Because of that, he has the power to mold us according to whatever plans and purpose he has for us. Human beings are nothing but clay relying on God the Potter's wonderful working to mold us and make us into vessels which are pleasing to him. As we yield to the Potter, He will make us strong, beautiful ready to fulfill a divinely ordained purpose which is at one with Him.

A careful study of Jeremiah 18:4-6 reveals to us how God puts his children on the potter's wheel to shape us as is pleasing to him. Verse 6 tells us that so far as we remain humble and obedient to God, He can do with us as the potter does with clay. Regardless of the mess, the disfigurement, the brokenness and the shapelessness, He can make us again into people of His choice. Our ability to surrender to God, as the clay remains flexible to the potter, will enable us to go through the changing scenes of life (potters wheel) and still come out as God's perfect gift, who is Christ.

It is believed that the potter's emotions during working times play a vital role in the making of the vessel. When the potter is in a good mood and high spirits, chances are the clay on the potter's wheel will always result in something delightful and beautiful. On the other hand, if the potter is aggrieved, no remarkable product will be made by his grieved and troubled hand. It is also believed that every vessel reveals the potter's heart.

Do not grieve the Holy Spirit of God, by whom you were sealed for the day of redemption.
Ephesians 4:30

The Holy Spirit, who is also God, is sensitive. He is not an active force as some people claim but He is gentle. We are the clay and God is the potter. He manifests his pottery duties through earthly fathers, priests, pastors etc. We should understand that in grieving the fathers and priests that God has given us, we could be putting ourselves in a very risky position where we could lose our God-given Grace to display His greatness, power and beauty through our lives to the world. Obey your leaders and submit to them, for they keep watch over your souls as those who will give an account.

Let them do this with joy and not with grief, for this would be unprofitable for you.
Hebrews 13:17

God's process of dealing with us and preparing us follows the same steps as that of the earthly potter in molding a pottery vessel: from the discovery of the clay through the developmental stages to its completion.

The Potters Wheel and Throwing Process

One of the most common methods potters use in creating objects out of clay is to use a potter's wheel. The entire process of forming a pot out of clay on the potter's wheel is generally called throwing. There are several steps within this process, such as centering, opening, throwing the walls, and finalizing the form. It is so amazing to see a lump of clay thrown on the potter's wheel ready to be molded according to the potter's plan; the potter spins the wheel from the base and then gently and skilfully molds the formless clay. The potter's physical and emotional composure cannot be ignored as he expectantly awaits the rough clay to rise with time. The shapeless clay gradually rises showing its promising beauty as the potter's amazing hands form it with care and one hundred percent uninterrupted attention.

To make a bigger vessel, the potter molds the upper part, the lower part and the other parts separately and then joins them carefully. The potter meticulously taps the vessel with his flat wooden tool to strengthen the joints, giving the bigger vessel a shape and to enhance its distinction and peculiarity. People who visit the potter and see the disjointed vessel often wonder what the potter is making i.e. what he intends the final product to be, its function and appearance, but it takes the potter to explain what is being made to the vigilant layman for greater appreciation. Finally, when all the different parts have been carefully put together and the big vessel, having gone through all of the potter's processes, is displayed or showcased, even people who have been around the potter will ask the potter how it arrived at the location. Others may ask when it was produced, and some may enquire whether it was imported. Then the potter will gently and calmly reply that that was the vessel that had been lying down in pieces in his workshop for years that some people had written off as a nuisance, useless and good for nothing. In fact, some may have even advised that it should be gotten rid of, but the potter had an undisclosed plan of greatness for it.

Beloved reader, every vessel that the potter forms whether big, medium, or small goes through the furnace fire. The purpose is not to destroy the vessel but to strengthen the vessel, making it strong so that it will not break easily when completed and is being used. It is the potter who decides the temperature of the fire and also the length of time the vessel should remain in the fire. The vessel never decides the type of fire it needs and how long it should stay in the fire. If the vessel is brought from the oven before the time scheduled for it, it will be incomplete and if sold it will not achieve the original purpose for which it was made. In other words, it cannot serve its life-giving purpose fully before it breaks and is destroyed.

Likewise, God deals with all his children regardless of how big their gift or anointing is. The Bible says God is not a respecter of persons. For us to be vessels that God will have confidence in, God the master potter, will take us through the same experience, he will lead us through the furnace fire to make us ready to be used for his own glory. Like the pot of clay, we do not decide how long we should be in the "baker's oven." It is God who decides the length of time and intensity of the heat.

Each vessel depending on its size and purpose, has a different time and heat level. The small and domestic pot or jar has a short baking time and the heat level is also not too high. However, when it comes to big industrial and commercial vessels, they are baked in big fire ovens called kilns and they stay in the fire for a longer period than all other small and medium-size purposed vessels.

Although we are one in Christ Jesus, not all of us serve the same purpose. Some are made to be leaders and some are made to be followers, some are made to be presidents and some are made to be citizens, some are made to be pastors and some are made to be congregational members. In other words, some are made for giant purposes and some are made for small purposes, and we cannot question our maker for making us who we are.

There are different tests for different professions and levels: all of us don't write the same test. It is inappropriate to make an accountant sit a test for medical doctors in the same way it is inappropriate for a tutor to make a primary school pupil sit the test for the secondary school pupil. The Bible says God is not unrighteous to allow us to be tempted above what we cannot afford, for with every test that comes our way God makes a way for us to escape.

When small and medium (weak) vessels go through the fire as the big and giant vessels, they get cracked and get broken. God will not allow a "baby or child" in the faith to go through the test and the affliction made for "fathers and leaders" of faith.

God permits fiery trials to come our way because it gives us the opportunity to be toughened and strengthened so that we can be used for his own purpose.

Dear reader, our attitudes during stormy times are essential in our molding and making.

But He knows the way I take; when He has tried me, I shall come forth as gold.
Job 23:10

Our attitudes during the furnace fire experience will determine whether we will last or perish with our God given-grace.

In this you greatly rejoice, even though now for a little while, if necessary, you have been distressed by various trials, so that the proof of your faith, being more precious than gold which is perishable, even though tested by fire, may be found to result in praise and glory and honor at the revelation of Jesus Christ.
1 Peter 1:6-7

God's message to us through the potter and the clay experience is amazing. A newly formed jar is weak and cannot be used until it has gone through the fire and is well baked. This special knowledge is to be considered and treasured.

The clay, having gone through all the potter's processes of becoming a vessel, becomes complete. All who see it appreciate its striking beauty, unquestionable durability and incomparable quality. They give credit to the potter for an outstanding work done and confess its beauty and marvelous appeal. It is the same to all the children of God. Having gone through successfully the dealings of God and still standing, all who see us manifesting the grace of the Christ with proven character and great success will confess the doings of the Lord. All men will then give glory to God alone.

Some old earthen wares or vessels having served all their purposes and having reached their life span because of their quality and durability, are kept at museums. Some are recycled for different artistic works and yet others get broken into pieces. Surprisingly, it has been discovered that those broken pieces of the jar are not counted as useless but still have useful purposes although they are at the end of their life spans. Some get used as a platform to produce high quality salt and others are used as a high quality floor and wall tiles to decorate mansions and palaces. This is an encouragement for any child of God who feels he is down and out. God still has great plans and purposes for all of us, for he says:

> *I know the thoughts I have towards you they are not the thoughts of evil but of peace to bring you to an expected end...*
>
> Jeremiah 29:11

As long as we remain the children of God even when the worst happens to us, God will still make the best out of us, for it is not over until it is over.

Chapter 2

Potters as Fathers

Chapter Two

POTTERS AS FATHERS

But now O LORD, you are our Father, We are the clay, and You our potter. And all of us are the work of Your hand.
                                            Isaiah 64:8

This tells us we are no more capable of molding ourselves than the clay and that we depend on God as our potter to make us what we want to be in this life. It begins with the potter at the potter's house. The potter is God and he manifests himself as the father who uses earthly vessels called fathers. A father is an idiom of originator or an inventor of anything new. In this sense, potters are fathers because they originate and they invent. In the book of Isaiah, chapter 68, verse 8 tells us that fathers are potters. Like a child to the father so is clay to the potter. The potter has an ability to take a piece of clay no matter how bad it might be and create something good out of it which will be useful: that is the job of fathers.

You cannot call yourself a potter or a father if you have not brought out anything useful. Every potter should be able to identify a raw material and develop it. Potters, like fathers, are owners of whatever they develop; it is not vessels which take the glory although they might be honored but the potter who invented the vessel who does. When men are saying how nice the vessel is, the sons don't take the glory, but give it to the fathers. Why? Because they know that all they are and possess is not their own, but has a source. So when the glory and honor comes, they give it back to their source, the fathers. They know it all started from there.

> *..see your good works, and glorify your Father who is in heaven.*
> Matthew 5:16

There is a Nigerian proverb that says *every river that forgets its source dries up.* Like clay in the hand of the potter, so are children in the hands of the fathers. We are all the handiworks of our fathers whether we believe it or not. The source of our success is God the potter.

The Potter's House is the House of the Lord

The potter's house is the potter's workshop which is the house of God. It is where the potter molds his craft. In Jerusalem it was situated at the southern part which is beyond the valley of Hinnom.

> *Then the LORD said to me, "Throw it to the potter, that magnificent price at which I was valued by them." So I took the thirty shekels of silver and threw them to the potter in the house of the LORD.*
> Zechariah 11:13

The potter's house is where all begins. It is the place where he forms all his vessels, so when any vessel the potter has formed develops a fault, this is where the vessel is taken for advice and possible restoration.

When the advice or the words of the potter concerning the broken earthen vessel are not adhered to or well taken the results will be a disaster because the vessel has made a horrible choice not to listen to his maker.

The potter's house is where the potter pours out his heart to the vessel he has made to form, reforms the broken ones, warns them of dangers ahead and makes heartfelt request to the vessels to hear and to follow his instructions and his engrafted word which is able to secure them in order to save them from being destroyed.

When the clay is marred, it is not thrown away: the clay is crushed together and then taken to the plate of wood on which he lays the clay to be molded or remolded with his fingers.

> *But the vessel that he was making of clay was spoiled in the hand of the potter; so he remade it into another vessel, as it pleased the potter to make.*
> Jeremiah 18:4

The word marred is translated from the Hebrew word *mishchath* which means to disfigure or corrupt. This tells us that when the earthen vessel becomes disfigured or corrupt, the potter still does not throw it away. It is the same: No matter how bruised, injured, disfigured or messed up we become, our potter and our father does not throw us away or neglect us or write us off. He sees an opportunity to speak his words of wisdom into our lives and then makes an ardent heartfelt request for us to listen to him while he is revealing to us the extent of our wounds and brokenness. Then he shows us how disfigured we have become, and then gives us the opportunity to listen to him in order to be healed, remolded and restored to the potter's design.

> *Can I not, O house of Israel, deal with you as this potter does?" declares the LORD. "Behold, like the clay in the potter's hand, so are you in My hand, O house of Israel.*
>
> Jeremiah 18:6

As the clay is soft in the hands of the potter while being molded into shape the potter finds good, so are we in the hands of God. He can make us and mold us into the design and purpose for his own pleasure if we shall remain humble and submissive to him.

In this message at the potter's house, the prophet Jeremiah was first called to observe the work of the potter as he forms them with his fingers on the wooden plate and he sees a vessel which was marred being made all over again into wonderful people.

In the house of God so far as we remain obedient and submissive to his will no situation nor condition will remain impossible, nothing will become too difficult for the lord to change, for he said, *"behold I am the lord the God of all flesh and is there anything too hard me?"*

The Chosen People

There are many different types of soil in the world, which may be good for different purposes, but only the clay is suitable for making pottery and therefore has been chosen by the potter for all his works, in the same manner the Lord has chosen Israel among many nations as his people. God told Abraham that his descendants shall be like the stars in the heaven and he also told Abraham that his descendants shall be like the sand at the seashore. The stars in the heaven and the sand at the seashore indicate his spiritual descendants and the natural descendants of Abraham respectively.

You did not choose Me but I chose you, and appointed you that you would go and bear fruit, and that your fruit would remain, so that whatever you ask of the Father in My name He may give to you.
John 15:16
But the Lord said to him, "Go, for he is a chosen instrument of Mine, to bear My name before the Gentiles and kings and the sons of Israel."
Acts 9:15

The Bible calls the church *ecclesia* meaning the called out ones for God's purposes

just as He chose us in Him before the foundation of the world, that we would be holy and blameless before Him In love
Ephesians 1:4

When the term "elect" is used theologically in the New Testament, it always refers to those who place their faith in Christ, chosen by God for a particular purpose. It could designate individual believers or the church collectively but never the world in general.

The Lord classifies Israel as clay in the hands of a potter because clay has the characteristics no other soil has. It has the features of meekness, submissiveness, bond and flexibility. These are the basic characteristics that the Lord requires from his people. This is one of the many reasons He chose clay when He was creating man in His image and likeness to rule and to dominate over all the earth. That is why He said *"as the clay is in the hands of the potter so are ye in my hands."* The above qualities are "must have" if you are a child of God.

The First is Bond

A bond is a unity force that is to join securely, as with glue. This is one major feature that the clay has that many of the soils in the world do not have. It has within it a quality of sticking together as one body with the help of water. That is why, of all the soil in the world, there is just one that the potter uses to form into vessels. Unity or togetherness is one of the qualities God cherishes.

> *The LORD said, "Behold, they are **one** people, and they all have the same language. And this is what they began to do, and now nothing which they purpose to do will be impossible for them."*
>
> Genesis 11:6

. . . So they are no longer two, but one flesh. What therefore God has joined together let no man separate."
                                        Matthew 19:6

Unity is oneness and oneness gives power and strength. You need oneness in order to be able to form a body or any organization.Genesis 11:1-7

In Genesis 11:6, God got his grammar right when he said behold the people is one and that nothing would be able to restrain them from what they have imagined doing.

The reason why the potter finds it possible to mold a vessel from clay is its unique quality to be able to join different pieces of clays together and then to form a uniform body. That is why God is able to bring different tribes, races, cultures, and nations together and then call it his people, his church or the body of Christ. There is no vessel that the potter would not be able to build with the clay if he wants to. That is why God said, "*Oh house of Israel cannot I do with you as this potter for as the clay is to the potter so are his people.*" For with God all things are possible.

Unity enhances success, achievement and possibility.

Behold, how good and how pleasant it is for brothers to dwell together in unity! It is like the precious oil upon the head, coming down upon the beard, Even Aaron's beard, coming down upon the edge of his robes. It is like the dew of Hermon Coming down upon the mountains

> of Zion; for there the LORD commanded the blessing—life forever.
> Psalm 133:1-3

Unity brings God's blessing and it pleases him!
Unity brings refreshment!
Unity, like the cord of three strands, cannot be broken easily!
Unity is strength!
Unity brings power!
Unity brings victories!
Unity is oneness!

To bond also means a binding agreement or covenant relationships. Metaphorically, God uses the scenario of the earthly potter and the clay as himself and Israel respectively. The earthly potter has a day-to-day relationship with the clay and so it is with God and his people. The potter has an imminent responsibility to turn the clay to a vessel fit for use by its master. So are we the sole responsibility of our maker the Lord. He will mold, bless us and make us great, a vessel of honor fit for his own purposes.

> *I will take note of you as you pass under my rod, and I will bring you into the bond of the covenant.*
> Ezekiel 20:37

Of all the nations of the earth, God chose Israel to have a covenant relationship with him. If they will obey him and walk in his statutes, he will fulfill the words and the promises of the covenant, as it is in Deuteronomy 28 from verse 1. If they will not walk in his statutes and obey him, then they will face an imminent destruction, as one breaks the potter's vessel that cannot be made whole again as stated in Jeremiah 19:1-13.

The Second is Flexibility

Another nature of clay that makes it suitable to be used by the potter is its flexibility, that is, its ability to be curved or turned to any direction or shape the potter sees fit for the design he has in mind for the vessel. Anything that is flexible is not rigid. In other words it is soft and it does not need force to be applied to it before it can be turned to any shape. Flexibility is a typical feature of clay that makes it different from other soil types. The clay, because of its flexible and soft nature does not have a "say" nor can it offer any suggestion to the potter when it is being molded but remains the dead clay which is at the mercy of the potter. Instead it "says" to the potter, I am all yours. I have surrendered 100% to your will, your design and to your purpose. Flexible clay is non-stubborn.

The soft and flexible nature of clay is another reason why God chose the clay for creating man in his own image and likeness and gave him authority and dominion over all his creation on earth and also chose the clay to symbolise Israel his chosen and elected covenant people. He said, *"As the clay is in the hands of the potter so are you in my hands,"* we, being the clay and the Lord being the potter. Our nature should be like that of the clay: We should be wholly submissive to him, we should yield to him, and we should die to our own will and live to fulfill his will. The Lord should be able to turn and curve us in any direction, to whichever shape, whenever, however, whatever and wherever, without us suggesting to Him our interest and will.

> *Woe to the one who quarrels with his Maker— An earthenware vessel among the vessels of earth! Will the clay say to the potter, "What are you doing?"Or the things you are making say, "He has no hands"?*
>
> Isaiah 45:9

This never happens with clay because of its typical character. If we are true people of God, there is no way we can be able to question our maker as to why he made us, who we are, and question the assignment he has given to us. The true clay turns in any direction the potter wants without breaking. It is in this same way that every true child of God should be able to carry out any assignment the Lord gives to him without turning away. That is why Jesus said in the book of John 10:27 "*My sheep hear My voice, and I know them, and they follow Me.*"

The true child of God's life is formed of three qualities: First is to Believe, which implies a life of complete and continued obedience. Second is to hear His voice, that indicates not hearers only, but doers of the word and able to take divine instructions without complaining. The third is to follow. This indicates not only the beginning of the Christian experience but a path to be continued daily and throughout our lives.

The Third is Meekness

The next nature of clay is its meekness. Meek is an adjective meaning quiet, soft, gentle, modest, humble, submissive, yielding, longsuffering, peaceful and ready to obey or submit to others or ready to serve. Meekness is a typical inbuilt quality of any good clay; it comes with it and you cannot separate this quality from it. Another reason why the potter uses clay is this quality. Because the physical clay used by the potter to make a vessel willingly submits and yields without being stiff to the potter and allows itself to be made to whatever vessel or shape the potter wants, it is the only ideal soil. God classifies his covenant people or children to be clay and no other soil because of this uniqueness that no other soil has.

The two greatest characters in the Bible possessed this quality, Moses and Christ. Moses is the example in the Old Testament. God required character and Jesus is the perfect example of the New Testament through his way of life.

Now the man Moses was very humble, more than any man who was on the face of the earth.
Numbers 12:3

"Take My yoke upon you and learn from me, for I am gentle and humble in heart, and YOU WILL FIND REST FOR YOUR SOULS."
Matthew 11:29

The above two, the greatest characters had this quality because they had the heart and the mind that willingly yielded and accepted God's will and desire without any resistance. These two characters were never self-willed, never had their own way or ideas or wishes, but with this nature of meekness they possessed they always said *"not my will but your will, oh God."* Posting the nature of meekness would enable you to put yourself in second place and submit yourself completely to serve and also to achieve what would be good for others.

Meekness is the opposite of self-will, self-interest and self-assertiveness. Although meekness might have "spineless" as a synonym, this is not a sign of weakness of character but it is a sign of strength, because it requires great self control to submit to others.

Chapter 3

The Potter's Three D's

Chapter Three

The Potter's Three D's

The potter's 3D forces are the only framework of the potter's industrial analysis and the strategies for development used by the potter. He uses the concept of God's dealings with man to build all his work. This 3D force determines the quality, attractiveness, usefulness and the permanency of the potter's vessel.

<u>Attractiveness</u> in this context refers to the overall purpose that the designed vessel will serve. This will cause people to buy it at whatever cost. It is unattractive vessels that fight in the public and compete in the marketplaces for acceptance and recognition.

There is a Ghanaian proverb, *a good bead speaks for itself* and there is an English proverb which says *an empty barrel makes the most noise*. For the unattractive vessel, the potter has to discount the value of the vessel and even with that the customers still bargain for further discount before buying it.

The true and the genuine anointing attracts, and so far as you have this Grace to minister to the needs of man, it does not matter where you are located. People will come to you as they went to John the Baptist because the grace and the anointing attract. People will never take into consideration how much it will cost them to have you to be a blessing to them, because the grace, the gifting and the anointing can never be compared to gold and silver; neither can it be purchased with them.

Those who do not have it make so much noise about having it and they even build monuments and merchandise the little grace they have. They impose their gifts and abilities on their subjects; also they try to manipulate others to get what they want. They always think of making profit and what they can get from others, giving no consideration to what they can also sacrifice and offer to satisfy the needy. They consider themselves and their needs before considering the Kingdom.

Quality in this context refers to the totality of features and the characteristics of the vessel or its services that demonstrate the ability to satisfy its stated or its implied needs. It also refers to the original, the prototype. The potter always has an objective to produce a first class, second-to-none earthen vessel that will serve and satisfy completely the needs of people without any problems or questions.

There is always one original but duplicates and copies are many. The potter, like any other manufacturer, does not produce copies but only originals. Copies are not valuable, not attractive and do not serve the original purpose well. A copy is second class and inferior and can be deceptive. Although it has the look or the outward appearance of the original product, it is far from it. It is cheap and low class, it does not have the true characteristics and features of the original and also no organization would want to be identified with it, even if its true owners are not known. It is a product manufactured to fail. It has no "father(s)" and as the saying goes *success has many fathers while failure is an orphan.* It is a product at risk!

The copies have never been through any of the processes that originals have been through. It might take years for an original product to come out with such an outstanding quality with striking beauty, but it would only take an instant, a moment, a minute, an hour or a day for the copy to be seen all over the place.

It takes years for an Army General to be trained to save and defend a nation but it takes a day for a rebel leader to emerge to destroy in the name of saving and defending. The imitations go through the microwave process (fast food) while the original goes through the furnace fire of the oven.

Beloved, it is the same with God since he only makes original and first class vessels to meet and satisfy completely the needs of humanity without any problems.

> *Every good thing given and every perfect gift is from above, coming down from the Father of lights...*
>
> James 1:17

God believes in perfection and because of that all the generals or the vessels that God has used in times past and is still using have the qualities, characteristics and features to satisfy the needs of man.

God makes us without any intention for us to fail although accidents do occur along the way. Any gift that has not **fully** been through God's process of making vessels might not be original but it might be an imitation. An imitation might look, act and talk like the true gift but it is far from being the original. Imitations are deceptive, they are immature, and you see them like a moving smoke. Suddenly, they seem to be everywhere at a time and they disappear just as they appeared (suddenly). Their lives and ministries are built on their charisma and some gift but not on grace and character.

The vessels which are not originals have neither mentors nor fathers, no one wants to be identified with them, they are vessels of casualty and they cannot be corrected. They go back to their vomit; they keep making the same mistakes over and over again. They have all the charisma but no character. They seem to have all that they want in a very short time but it does not last because they do not know the cost and the value of what they possess.

Usefulness. This talks of how well the vessel that the potter makes achieves the purpose it is made for or the quality of the vessel being useful. The potter makes different vessels for different purposes and he intends that all the vessels he makes are used well and fulfill all the original purposes for which they are made.

Characteristics of a Useful Vessel

Useful vessels are those vessels which have been through all the required processes and also withstood the extreme firing processes and are giving a pure pinging sound.

- A useful vessel is a vessel which is empty.
- A useful vessel is the vessel which has been completely worked on by the potter.
- A useful vessel is a vessel which does not have deficiencies or blemishes both inside and outside.
- It is a vessel which has a larger capacity.
- A useful vessel might be beautiful, and also might be a wise vessel, but ultimately the useful vessel needs to be well designed for its intended use.

God also uses the same criteria when he picks up a vessel to use for his own purposes. All of us are vessels God can use if we are proper, that is, if we have allowed ourselves to be molded all by Him. We can be more useful if our vessels have big capacity but we would be less useful if our capacity is limited. If we empty ourselves, and open up our hearts to the Lord, we can be used for greater works.

To be used for greater and more honorable purposes we need to have a pure and open heart, the heart that seeks after the Lord and also we need to work on ourselves daily. If we do not work on ourselves daily, God cannot use us much. The more we work out, the more we expand and the more we expand, the bigger our capacity becomes and the bigger our capacity becomes, the more we can be filled with the living waters. We can use examples of two different vessels of different sizes. If we do not work out daily to develop ourselves we will remain small vessels; can someone put water into the small vessel? The answer is yes, pure and good water can be put into this vessel but how many people can drink from it and how many people can be supplied with fresh and living water from this vessel? A few can because it has a small capacity and it is limited. If you are loose and will not work on yourself and perfect yourself then your ministry will be a vessel with little capacity. You would give living water to people but how much and how many? However, it all starts small and becomes big with time; that is what nature has provided. We all grow. The small vessel might have the same content as the big vessel but still cannot be compared to what the bigger vessel can be used to do and achieve. The big vessel sees more fulfillment and is used to serve big occasions. The number of people the big vessel can reach and satisfy in a short and limited period of time, the small vessel cannot.

To become a bigger vessel is a choice one has to make, and so is it a choice to become a vessel of honor fit for the master's use.

> *But in a great house there are not only gold and silver vessels, but also wooden and earthen; and some to honor, and some to dishonor. If therefore one shall have purified himself from these, [in separating himself from them], he shall be a vessel to honor, sanctified, serviceable to the Master, prepared for every good work.*
>   2 Timothy 2:21, Darby Translation

To become a big vessel in the hands of the Lord does not come cheap; it requires hard work from the individual. It demands vigorous and continuous spiritual exercise which will develop a strong spirit. One would ask what all this workout and spiritual exercise consists of. They consist of loyalty to the visionary you are following, willingness to carry out menial jobs in the church or serving, prayer and fasting, studying and researching the word of God regularly, outreaching and witnessing, being regular at church, being committed, devoted and consistent to your leader's vision etc.

A Useful Vessel is a Clean Vessel

If we become one with the world and think and act like them, we cannot expect the Lord to use us. Dear reader, we need to be sanctified inside and outside if we want to be used by God to minister life to others. As the saying goes: *"No one gives water to a cherished guest from a dirty cup."* It has to be clean both inside and outside and look presentable before it can be used.

The scripture even says we do not put new wine into an old bottle. It does not matter how pure the water is; if it is being served from a contaminated vessel, the water will also be contaminated and it will not be fit for drinking. It does not matter how much gift one might have. If he is not morally straight, the gift will be affected.

The Bible says *even if you speak with the tongues of angels and can move mountains, if you do not have love you are nothing.*

As Jesus asked *"Who do men say I am?"* No one said anything negative or bad about him. It should be the same for all of us who want to be used by

God. We should have good testimonies from the people we are being a blessing to. No matter how much anointing and the grace you might have, if men do not accept you, you cannot make an impact on them and cannot be a blessing to them because God does not force anyone to accept and receive anyone. Once men refuse to accept you, your gift is finished because we do not minister to angels but we minister to man for God's Glory. The scripture says Jesus could not perform any miracle in Nazareth because of their unbelief.

There was a great and respectable man of God who was once invited as a guest to minister in one of the largest churches in Africa. The program and all the arrangements were made, but just a few days before the commencement of this great program, there were rumors and questions about his spirituality in the media and immediately he was removed from the program.

Nobody wants to associate with a gift which has moral deficiencies, nor would like to be identified with charisma without character. Once the vessel is dented or has some blemishes, it loses it original value and worth and in most cases its useful life span comes to an end. If we want to be vessels serviceable to the master and prepared for every good work we should hold up our integrity in high esteem.

Permanency

Permanency of the vessel being used speaks of the vessel's continuing or enduring without change in condition or purpose with time. Every potter who designs a vessel builds the vessel with the quality that will make it serve for a period of time and mostly not for a short period. The permanency talks about its lifelong serving, enduring accident, mishandling, or abuse, without breaking or failing. For this reason, the potter avoids shortcut processes or easy and quick methods of molding the vessel. There is a saying: "*Anything worth doing is worth doing well.*"

Right from the start, the potter adopts quality processes and standards which are hard measures to ensure that the vessel being molded will be able to withstand pressure, shock, accident, abuse, mishandling, etc. These quality measures will increase the lifespan of the vessel, and also distinguish it from the many imitations.

Although no one is indispensable, God never intends to use us for a short period and then dump us. God believes in consistency and continuity and that is why he promised David he would never cease to have a man on the throne. God never intends for the men he is using to fail; because of that he never uses cheap vessels. That is the reason it cost him all that he had, I mean his only begotten son, to come and die for us so that he will get for himself many sons like his own son Jesus to accomplish his will and plan on earth. God intends that every vessel he designs and makes for his own purpose serves throughout the number of years he has designed it for, that it be used without failing or dying a natural death, and to accomplish the purposes for which he made it. As Dr. Morris Cerullo always puts it, "*God is a God of plan, design, purpose, and objectivity.*"

God pours himself into the vessels that He uses, so that He will be directing and guiding us from within. He prepares us and fortifies us to be able to withstand evil days, i.e. persecutions, trials and hardships, which can cause us to fail our God-given purposes on earth.

Because God believes in quality, He does not use people who have not been through His processes; I mean instant vessels. Instead He takes time and years to prepare his vessels. Instant and microwave ministries and gifts come all of a sudden and they are everywhere in a short time and they seem to have it all, but nature uses time to prove whether they are of God or they are imitations. They do not stand the test of time, their gift and ministries do not last because they are built on earthly treasures and talents but not on the Word of God. The scriptures say, *He that is born of God overcomes the world.*

The Potter's Framework

The 3D forces are the potter's framework or the potter's logical model which he follows in order to get a useful completed vessel. The 3D's stand for Discovery, Development and Dispatch. The 3D stages really define the whole duties of every true potter.

For you to be a potter, you have to be an expert in discovering a good clay from mud, developing the clay to become a useful vessel, and then dispatching the vessel to the right place where it will be used for the very purpose for which it was designed. A potter must also be able to mend broken vessels to be useful again. Potters are the symbol of fathers, priest and mentors. They aim at saving souls, healing and restoring the broken. It does not come easily for anyone to be able to get any of these titles. The person should be able to birth and identify a gift or a raw talent, develop the individual through a series of life mentoring procedures and disciplines to serve and also to become useful to satisfy needs and wants. The father or the mentor should be able to have 100% confidence and utmost good faith in the individual he has trained that he will fulfill and achieve the very purpose he has developed him for without failing.

THE FIRST D STANDS FOR DISCOVERY

To discover means to find a thing or to find out something previously unknown or unrecognized.
"He reveals mysteries from the darkness and brings the deep darkness into light." Job 12:22
This scripture talks about God the master potter bringing to light or revealing what is hidden or what no one has knowledge of. The first step in making a useful vessel is to obtain the proper clay.

The proper clay that the potter uses is mostly not discovered in town centers or cities, but in places which are far away from home, remote and depleted places. In some cases, clay is discovered in thick forest, in places that never become developed, waterlogged and mosquito-infested, the places that never become part of town and country planning developmental projects, an obscure place, a jungle, a place that never becomes a tourist attraction, a rejected and dejected place. It is from these very abandoned places that the potter discovers his treasures and then develops them to become useful vessels of honor which are so valuable that they will be needed by men and women of honor: kings, queens, presidents, secretary generals, CEO's etc.

> *For while we were still helpless, at the right time Christ died for the ungodly. For one will hardly die for a righteous man; though perhaps for the good man someone would dare even to die. But God demonstrates His own love toward us, in that while we were yet sinners, Christ died for us. Much more then, having now been justified by His blood, we shall be saved from the wrath of God through Him. For if while we were enemies we were reconciled to God through the death of His Son, much more, having been reconciled, we shall be saved by His life. And not only this, but we also exult in God through our Lord Jesus Christ, through whom we have now received the reconciliation.*
> Romans 5:6-11

In the same way, Jesus did not come for the self righteous but for the downtrodden, for sinners, the poor, the broken, the homeless and the captives.

> *"THE SPIRIT OF THE LORD IS UPON ME, BECAUSE HE ANOINTED ME TO PREACH THE GOSPEL TO THE POOR. HE HAS SENT ME TO PROCLAIM RELEASE TO THE CAPTIVES, AND RECOVERY OF SIGHT TO*

THE BLIND, TO SET FREE THOSE WHO ARE OPPRESSED, TO PROCLAIM THE FAVORABLE YEAR OF THE LORD."
                                         Luke 4:18-19

The Lord picked us from the dark world and brought us into the kingdom of light, from slavery to become sons and heirs of the kingdom. The songwriter says, "he took my feet from the miry clay and set it on the solid rock to stay, precious blood washed my sins away, he is my Savior, my friend and my Lord." It is believed treasures are hidden in the darkness. Moses was hidden in the very house of Egypt when male sons were being killed and Jesus was also hidden in Egypt when Herod was looking for him, and the scriptures even say out of Egypt I will call my son. The very place that miners discover and mine their treasures in various parts of the world are places no one would ever like to live except those who know what treasure is there. In the same way, if you are not wise, you will despise in your heart at the first glance the very people that God has deposited his treasure in.

Potters see things differently from ordinary people. When people are seeing clay as messy, useless and valueless, the potter sees from that same clay which has been despised, a vessel that men of higher standard would bargain for. The potter sees a vessel that will cost hundreds of thousands of dollars. The potter sees a vessel that will be highly sought after by kings and royals who will need it to decorate their palaces and also use it to serve their cherished guests.

In the same way, Jacob the father of the tribes of Israel saw Joseph his son different from his own brothers. Joseph's brothers saw him as little and useless, but his father saw a king and a priest. Because of that, while he was young his father decorated him with the coat of many colors which was the prescribed regalia for kings and priests. The potter will always agree with the words of Job in Job 8:7 *"Though your beginning was insignificant, yet your end will increase greatly."*

People said, "Can anything good come out of Nazareth?" but it is there where Jesus the Christ started and came from to be the greatest king of all time. When the family of David saw him as the shepherd, Samuel saw a giant slayer and a king. God hides his treasures in unlikely vessels. It is our duty to discover them.

The potter is not moved by where the clay is and how it is looking, but he looks into the future of the remote and the ugly clay and sees a completed and a refined valuable vessel of honor that will be used to serve kings and the VIPs, and then tells himself, it does not matter how much it will cost me to get this vision and accomplish this mission; I will go for it.

In the same manner, it does not matter to God how damaged our background is, or how filthy and dirty we are or how bad our sins are. He looks beyond our faults and sinful states and meets our needs. That is why the Bible says that *while we were yet sinners Christ died for us* and the scripture says also in Isaiah:

"Come now, and let us reason together", says the LORD, "Though your sins are as scarlet, they will be as white as snow; though they are red like crimson, they will be like wool."
Isaiah 1:18

God sees a slave who has become a son, he sees a prisoner who has become a prime minister, he sees a poor man who has become wealthy, he sees a murderer who has become the great apostle, he sees the chief sinner who has become the greatest evangelist winning souls into the kingdom of our Lord and Savior Jesus.

Baptism

It is believed that the best kind of clay to work with is that which is found at the bottom of a lake. It has been soaked by the water for a long period of time. If you tried to scoop it up while it was still soaking in the water you would grab a mixture of sand and clay, which would be useless. You must first wait for the lake to dry up because during the process of drying the clay separates from the sand. To know where the clay is, you must look for it carefully. It sits on top of the gravel, cracked and cupped from the shrinkage. As each irregular disc of clay is gathered, the potter brushes off any sand clinging to the bottom of the clay disc. If the potter is too impatient to brush off the clingy sand, since the clay is moist on the bottom, it means there will be a lot of work later getting rid of the sand.
The above paragraph talks about water baptism. Water baptism is one of the bases of our whole

Christian life and the gateway to our new life. Through it we are freed from sin. Jesus authorized it in Matthew 28:19. . .*baptizing them in the name of the Father and the Son and the Holy Spirit,* and also in the book of Acts 10 when Peter went to the house of Cornelius the Gentile and preached to them, the Holy Ghost fell on them. In verse 47 it was asked, *Can any man forbid water that these should not be baptized, which have received the Holy Ghost as well as we?*

Baptism is also an expression of repentance, complete surrender and total submission. John the Baptist came and that was his main ministry. Individuals who have repented and totally and completely surrendered to God are the people (clay) that are ready to be molded by God (potter) into vessels that can be used for his honorable purposes. The clay (people) that is found at the bottom of the lake represents the people who have been baptized in water. Baptism by immersion is a symbol of burying the old nature and coming out of the water is also a symbol of resurrection.

> *Or do you not know that all of us who have been baptized into Christ Jesus have been baptized into His death? Therefore we have been buried with Him through baptism into death, so that as Christ was raised from the dead through the glory of the Father, so we too might walk in newness of life.*
> Romans 6:3-13

It is the clay that has separated from sand that is pure and unadulterated that the potter is looking for to use to mold a vessel of honor, and not the clay that is mixed with sand. No good potter would use clay that has some amount of sand mixed into it to mold into a vessel, because he knows the outcome. The vessel cannot stand any heat, not to mention fire. It would crack and break. It does not matter to the potter the length of time it takes him to separate the sand from the clay. He will be patient, or otherwise he will spend all the rest of his precious time on repairing or mending a vessel that can never be made whole again.

Dear reader, the individuals that the Lord is looking for to make them instruments and vessels of honor are those who have no friendship with the world, people who have put to death, crucified and buried their old sinful natures, I mean Christians who are completely separated and saved from sin and having no more connection with it than a dead body has with a departed spirit.

The Lord will never make anyone who is still living in bondage to his past life an instrument or a vessel of honor. It is simply not possible. Such vessels would fail and it would bring a reproach and embarrassment to God and his kingdom and they can never be made whole until the first thing is done, that is the separation from the sinful nature.

THE SECOND D STANDS FOR DEVELOPMENT

After the potter has discovered and mined the proper clay, the next thing he would do is to develop and design the clay to become a useful vessel. He does not leave the clay to develop itself in the jungle or the deprived place he discovered it.

Development is defined as significant consequences of events, occurrences or change. It is also an act of improving something. It can be defined, too, as the process in which something passes through degrees to a different state. It is also used to mean disciple.

Just as clay needs a potter to mold it to become a useful vessel so does every individual need a father or a mentor to become a gift and a blessing. Apart from God who has no beginning and ending and who cannot be made by anyone, all of us have to be made, we cannot just arrive, some one has to take us there. We need fathers to make us. A father, like a football coach, may not be able to score a goal, but can make someone a world number one top player.

THE THIRD D STANDS FOR DISPATCH

Dispatch is defined as: to send away towards a designated goal or to complete or to carry out specific duties. After the potter has discovered the clay and has developed the clay to become a beautiful vessel with a purpose, he does not store the vessel in his workshop. Instead, he dispatches it. That is, he puts it on sale to send the vessel away to individuals who may need it either to serve their guests or to use as a decoration for their palaces, temples, houses or for any other purpose.

Dear reader, this is how God deals with us. After he saved us, he disciples us through natural fathers, mentors, teachers and priests, etc., to be formed and to be molded to his desired purposes. He sends us away to meet the needs of the world.

For the anxious longing of the creation waits eagerly for the revealing of the sons of God.
                                    Romans 8:19

The truth is that no father or teacher will keep his son or his pupil forever. There comes a time that the baby boy is no longer a baby but grows into man who leaves his father's house, cleaves to his wife and then they also start a family. Or there comes a time that after the student has graduated to become a medical doctor, his teachers do not keep him in the school, but they send him out into the world to save lives.

Folks, as the discovery stage is as important as the developing stage, so is the developing stage as important as the dispatch stage. All the three come together as a package. No one (unless discovered) can be sent (dispatched) to accomplish any great purpose or assignment if that individual has not been prepared (developed). I have a very simple mathematical equation for this. Purpose-Preparation=Failure.

When we check history books from the days of the Bible till now, there is no general or hero who did not start out as an apprentice. All of those God used for greater purposes, he first put through apprenticeship before they all came out to achieve greatness. For example, Abraham met Melchisedec and was blessed by him. Isaac was mentored by Abraham his father, Isaac blessed Jacob, Moses was groomed by Pharaoh to be king, and learned leadership skills by serving Jethro. David became the servant and armor bearer of Saul. The disciples were trained and taught by Christ himself. Saul, before he became Paul the greatest apostle, first sat and learned at the feet of the apostles for many years. We should not ever forget this. Great and Powerful Men in history and in present times did not seek to be Great and Powerful but they sought to SERVE.

Folks, without fathers and mentors our lives become an experiment and a project bound to fail. Let us note this carefully. *It's all right to leave from your father's house because nature demands that, but it's so wrong to break away from your father's house. It often ends with a curse.*

Again, as we go out there to fulfill the great commission and pursue our dreams, we will never be without casualty. Sometimes we may fall, at other times we may be injured very badly, because the world out there is a battlefield.

For we wrestle not against flesh and blood, but against principalities, against powers, against the rulers of the darkness of this world, against spiritual wickedness in high places.

Ephesians 6:12

There is a famous Chinese proverb that says *fallen leaves always return to their root*. When we get injured or broken, it is our father's house where we were made that we need to get back to for restoration, comfort and healing. However, if we left there fighting everyone including our Pastors and finding 101 faults with everything including our Pastor's pet then we will never be able to return, when we get broken, for solace, comfort and healing and we will die bleeding.

Section II

The 7 Stages of Development

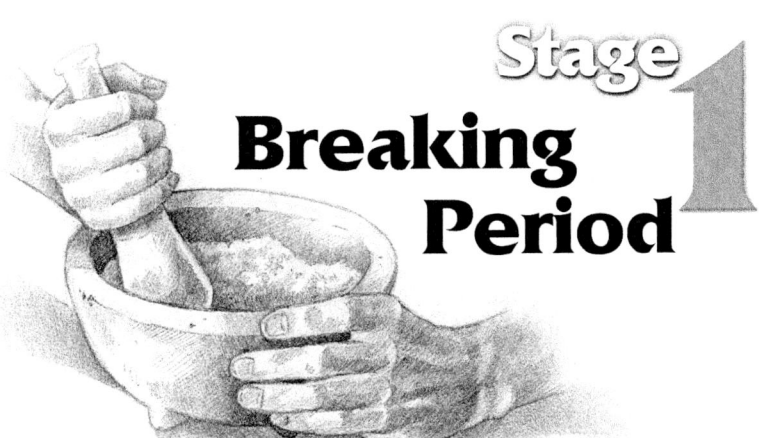

Stage 1
Breaking Period

There are Seven Stages of developing clay into a useful vessel. According to theologians the number seven stands for perfection, completion or wholeness. For the clay to become a useful vessel, it has to go through seven different stages of change.

1st STAGE OF DEVELOPMENT - MORTAR AND PESTLE METHOD

At the potter's house, all clay collected is broken into small pieces and is crushed together in a large barrel. In Africa, there is a method the potter adopts when he wants to crush the clay; it is called the mortar and pestle method. In this method, the potter places some of the disc of clay collected into the mortar and then uses the pestle to pound it several times in order to break all non clay particles that are found in the clay and also to get the clay to become softer.

The pestle can be likened to the rod of correction. It stands for love, chastisement, rebuke, correction and discipline. Fathers and teachers who are our potters use the rod on us, not because they do not love us, but because they have our success at heart.

He who withholds his rod hates his son, but he who loves him disciplines him diligently.
                              Proverbs 13:24

The potter uses the pestle and the mortar method because it is an effective way of breaking the non-clay elements found in the clay which will prevent the clay from being molded into a useful vessel of honor.

On the lips of the discerning, wisdom is found, but a rod is for the back of him who lacks understanding.
                              Proverbs 10:13

Do not hold back discipline from the child, although you strike him with the rod, he will not die. You shall strike him with the rod and rescue his soul from Sheol.
                              Proverbs 23:13-14

There comes a point during the pounding process that some of the clay may fall out of the mortar because the potter is hitting is so hard and vigorously, but the potter collects all those particles and puts them back into the mortar again and continues to pound it severely. By the time the potter is finished with that section of pounding, you will be amazed to know that some of the clay particles will fall out again with some of the non-clay particles, while some of the non-clay particles will remain throughout the pounding process.

In the same manner, when we are going through our period of discipline by our fathers, some of us take it personally and get offended because we think our fathers are being political, they dislike us and do not have good plans for us, and we tend to leave our father's house (change churches). Some may even stop going to the church altogether and others even refuse to get involved in Christianity again.

In some cases, the fathers bring us back again into our previous positions and then continue to hit us with the rod so that we will change and get rid of the bad habits that have become part of us and would prevent us from being made into what God wants us to be. At the end of the day, some get really offended and backslide, others change churches, and still others stay in the church only to cause problems.

Offend comes from two words: that is **off** and **end**. Whenever we get offended as a result of hating discipline, we switch **off** ourselves from the source of life and we **end** it pre-maturely. This results in some dying a natural death and, of course, prematurely. With others, their gift and their talent die. In other words, they stop functioning because they have been switched off from the main source because of offence.

Some people change fathers, and others also make themselves fathers when they are not fathers. Calling someone a father who never contributed to your upbringing and does not know how you started can be an error. Also making yourself a father when you have not been fathered makes you a rebel leader.

FATHERS WHO FAIL TO CORRECT THEIR SONS

Proverbs 13:24 tells us that *he who fails to discipline his son does not love him, but he who disciplines,* chastises rebukes and corrects his son has his future in mind and loves him.

There are many examples in the Bible of fathers who failed to correct and discipline their sons and their end result.

Eli

> *"Then bring near to yourself Aaron your brother, and his sons with him, from among the sons of Israel, to minister as priest to Me— Aaron, Nadab and Abihu, Eleazar and Ithamar, Aaron's sons.*
>
> Exodus 28:1

Aaron, his sons and their descendants were the only family in Israel consecrated into the office of the priest. Eli, being the descendant of Aaron, was the fifteenth judge and the seventh high priest of Israel. He judged for 40 years. At the end of his service as high priest and judge of Israel, his sons who were Hophni and Phinehas were to continue the priesthood office by divine order. These two were to be groomed by their father to take on the highest office in Israel. However, these two, in the process of them being molded into useful vessels to honor God, did not conform to the priestly rules and regulations and started leading lives of sin. Their father, the high priest, knew but failed to charge them for their wrongdoing and also failed to discipline them.

> *For I have told him that I am about to judge his house forever for the iniquity which he knew,*

> because his sons brought a curse on themselves and he did not rebuke them. Therefore I have sworn to the house of Eli that the iniquity of Eli's house shall not be atoned for by sacrifice or offering forever.
> 1 Samuel 3:13-14

In 1 Samuel 2:12-17, the scriptures describe them as the sons of Belial. That means they chose to serve the devil and they committed many sins against the Lord and refused to repent even when their misdeeds became known to everyone.

Eli, being a judge, a father, a potter, training and molding his sons to become the high priests of Israel, refused to discipline and suspend his sons from their offices as priests. He neither used the rod of chastisement on them nor did he openly confront and rebuke those while they were bringing reproach to the ministry of the high priest. So the Lord judged the whole house of Eli. The two sons died and never became high priests and the priesthood office was switched to another family, the family of Levi. A successful man leaves an inheritance for his children's children, but Eli could not be one because his children failed.

Samuel

The second character I will discuss with you is the prophet Samuel.

> And it came about when Samuel was old that he appointed his sons judges over Israel. Now the name of his firstborn was Joel, and the

> *name of his second, Abijah; they were judging in Beersheba. His sons, however, did not walk in his ways, but turned aside after dishonest gain and took bribes and perverted justice.*
>
> 1 Samuel 8:1-3

The scripture tells us when the prophet was old, he started grooming his sons Joel and Abijah to rule in Israel by their system of government, which was theocracy, so he started by making them judges in a small town called Beersheba. In the process of time, the sons of Samuel who were to become judges in all of Israel refused to judge themselves. Therefore they started walking in sin and engaging in all kinds of greed and living dishonest lives. Their father Samuel, being a judge, did not judge or discipline them. They continued operating in their office without any suspension or being brought to book. They still had their freedom despite the elders of Israel bringing to the notice of Samuel the misdeeds of his sons. Because Samuel failed in his responsibility as a father, mentor and a potter to use the rod on his sons, he was denied the joy of seeing his sons taking after him and his sons never became the vessels God would use to rule his people.

Stage 2

Separation/ Elimination Period

THE 2ND STAGE OF MOLDING – FILTERING/SIEVING

At this stage, after the potter has discovered the proper clay, has collected and broken it into pieces and crushed them, he takes the small pieces of the dry clay and grinds them across a coarse screen to separate it. This is what is termed as filtering or sieving.

Filtering the clay is clarifying the clay prior to the formation stage. The purpose of this is to remove all non-clay particles or elements from the mass of clay. If these are not found and removed, they will either prevent the clay from being molded into a vessel or cause a real problem for the vessel which would be made. It would fail and not be able to serve fully its purpose and that would be a discredit to the potter.

God expects fathers and mentors to deal with their children in the same way. At this stage, the fathers set an eagle eye on the children that they are grooming in order to spot any strange character or attitudes which their children might develop in the process of their upbringing.

At this time, it looks like the fathers are being too picky and too critical. I mean that they adopt the constructive criticism method, they seem not to notice our early achievement or to be too happy about our early successes, but are quick to identify what we have done wrong and it looks like they are fault-finding professionals. They seem not to give us any breathing space when we do not go right, they highlight it, talk about it, and bring it to the attention of all who matter and sometimes they would even take you to disciplinary hearing and suspension follows. If we are not wise, sometimes outsiders will make us think our fathers do not like us and will suggest we rebel against them because they do not have the slightest idea what our fathers are up to.

The Big Red Tree

There is a story about a massive redwood tree that had survived some 400 years in one of America's national forests. This ancient tree had survived 14 separate strikes by lightning; it had survived countless earthquakes, storms, floods and other violent natural disasters. Yet one day, without warning, this massive towering old tree came crashing to the ground with a tremendous thud. No bolt of lightning was responsible, no overzealous lumberjack had felled it. It came crashing to the ground for no apparent reason. On closer inspection, investigators discovered why this old tree had died. Tiny beetles had found their way inside its trunk and had begun eating away its life giving fibres, weakening this giant tree from the inside out.

Just imagine; what many lightning bolts, horrendous storms and earthquakes could not do was easily accomplished over the passage of time by a handful of small insects. In much the same way, great gifts and abilities which, when nurtured, can affect and serve nations and high dignitaries are floored and made useless by small, seemingly insignificant bad and weak attitudes which we did not let go.

Just as those small and insignificant beetles found access to the tender core of the huge 400-year-old redwood, so do small and insidious sins creep into our lives for the purpose of destroying our foundations, breaking and tearing apart our ministries and gifting and crashing to ground zero the monument and the good name that our fathers have taken many years to build.

Although every father knows that the present is as important as the future, they will not be satisfied by the present successes because it is the future glory they are looking for.

Stage 3

Oneness

THE 3ᴿᴰ STAGE OF MOLDING A VESSEL

    The potter, after discovering the proper clay, collecting it, breaking and crushing it into pieces and grinding the dry clay across a coarse screen to separate it from the non-clay particles, moves to a different process. The clay drops into a different barrel while the grit, sand and gravels remain on the screen. The potter has to constantly take the debris and dump it into a trash container. Then the clay is rubbed by hand across a fine screen to sieve the clay into a fine powder. The potter then adds water to the barrel of clay, but the clay powder will not absorb the water because the clay particles are flat so the water just runs off the little platelets. The potter must now reach into the barrel up to his elbow and mix the water in by squishing the clay and the water between his fingers. Water is added in this way until the clay's consistency is like peanut butter.

    Beloved, it is the same process God takes us through. The potter adds water to the barrel of clay and mixes the water in by squishing the clay and the water between his fingers. Water stands for life, which is the very nature of God, and the clay represents man. For God to make us in his likeness, to be a life-giving spirit, to be a vessel to offer life and to meet the needs of humanity, God takes our nature and then separates it from that of the world. He then pours out his spirit without measure into us which is the water and then squishes us and the spirit together with his own hand until we become one with his spirit, and possess the very nature and the abilities of Christ, so that when he sees us he sees himself and when we are squeezed, the content that comes is the very nature of God.

Oneness

Food is for the stomach and the stomach is for food, but God will do away with both of them Yet the body is not for immorality, but for the Lord, and the Lord is for the body. Now God has not only raised the Lord, but will also raise us up through His power. Do you not know that your bodies are members of Christ? Shall I then take away the members of Christ and make them members of a prostitute? May it never be! Or do you not know that the one who joins himself to a prostitute is one body with her? For He says, "THE TWO SHALL BECOME ONE FLESH." But the one who joins himself to the Lord is one spirit with Him.
1 Corinthians 6:13-17

In reference to the word of God, oneness with the spirit means the state of being absolutely and indivisibly one with the spirit. As Jesus Christ has said, *whoever sees me sees the father* because the father is in him and he is in the father, which is why He said I and my father are one. Before we can be molded as a vessel and be used for greater works, we have to come to that level of oneness with the spirit and with Christ that is what we call the third realm experience. I mean the holy of holiest experience; that is when and where there is none of the flesh but all of Christ. At that level, there is no struggling between the flesh and the spirit; it is when the curtain that divides the temple has been torn down. It is where Christ rules completely. The individual has fully and completely surrendered to Christ. It is the place that Apostle Paul reached in life when he said, *the life that I live it is not me but Christ.*

In the potter's house, we have reached the stage where and when the potter mixes the water in by squishing the clay and the water between his fingers until the clay absorbs so much water that it becomes like peanut butter. As soon as the potter gets the texture of the clay to become like peanut butter, he tells himself that every design is possible and, at that time, whatever size and shape he wants to mold it, be it big, small or medium, is possible.

In God's dealing with us, as soon as we get to the stage where we have become like Christ and are one with the spirit, there is no purpose or assignment he is not able to prepare us to fulfill. Everything becomes possible because, at that time, he replaces our weakness with his strength and his grace becomes sufficient for us and we become his representatives on earth. This is the very stage the apostle Paul got to when his shadows were healing the sick and aprons from him were being used to cast out devils.

For if we have become united with Him in the likeness of His death, certainly we shall also be in the likeness of His resurrection.
                                    Romans 6:5

At this stage of oneness we think, talk and act like Jesus because at this stage it is no longer us living, but Christ.

In the New Testament, oneness with the spirit is strictly differed from uniting with the spirit. Unity is formed by many people coming together, whereas oneness is the one entity of the spirit within us and making us one with Him. In Ephesians 4:3, we read *being diligent to preserve the unity of the Spirit in the bond of peace.*

This oneness is called the oneness of the spirit; the oneness of the spirit is actually the spirit himself. In the illustration of the electricity and light, the oneness of electricity is electricity itself. There is not another element apart from the electricity itself. In the same principle, our oneness with the spirit is not something apart from the spirit. The spirit within us is the very life-giving spirit, so automatically we also become life-giving spirit vessels and we move with the assignment of giving life to dead conditions and situations.

Canvas or Stage 4

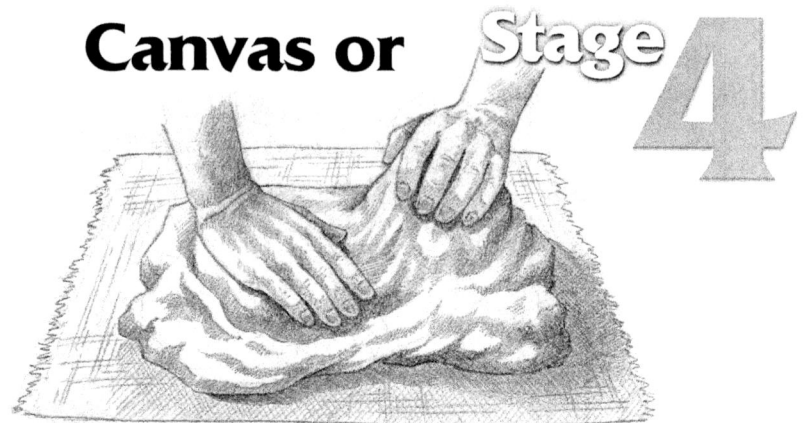

Upper Room Experience

THE 4TH STAGE OF MOLDING IS BAPTISM

At this stage, after the potter has finished squishing the clay and the water between his fingers, water is added until the clay's consistency is like peanut butter (oily). The clay is then scooped up and laid out on a canvas to absorb the excess water.

This stage signifies when we have received Jesus Christ as our Lord and Savior and the Lord has joined us to be one with him. He first begins to fill us with his nature till we are completely transformed to his nature. It is like peanut butter which is the oil and that symbolizes the anointing. It is only when our nature becomes like peanut butter that God can begin to mold us to any shape and to any size without any difficulty.

It is believed that when the consistency of the clay is like peanut butter, the clay is then scooped up and laid out on a canvas to absorb the excess water. This talks about the upper room experience preceding the Holy Ghost baptism in the book of the Acts of the Apostles.

> *Gathering them together, He commanded them not to leave Jerusalem, but to wait for what the Father had promised, "Which," He said, "you heard of from Me; for John baptized with water, but you will be baptized with the Holy Spirit not many days from now."*
> Act 1:4-5

John the Baptist baptized with water and he introduced another baptizer who is Jesus Christ who baptizes with the Holy Ghost and fire. In the scenario where the clay is being scooped up and laid out on a canvas to absorb excess water, the prepared clay is us and being scooped up is being ordered to remain in a particular place. The canvas is a tent that is the upper room, the absorbing of excess water is the outpouring of the Holy Spirit on us.

> *When the day of Pentecost had come, they were all together in one place. And suddenly there came from heaven a noise like a violent rushing wind, and it filled the whole house where they were sitting. And there appeared to them tongues as of fire distributing themselves, and they rested on each one of them. And they were all filled with the Holy Spirit and began to speak with other tongues, as the Spirit was giving them utterance.*
> Act 2:1-4

Baptism comes from the Greek word *Baptiso* which means to dip. Baptiso is an old word which was commonly used by fabric dyers of the olden days. Today it is most often used for religious purposes only. In the olden days, they took the plain cloth and the process of lowering the cloth into the dye is what they called baptiso meaning baptism. When the cloth is fully immersed into the dye and is brought up from the dye we realize that there has been a 100% transformation, the cloth is fully soaked by the dye, the cloth drips the excess dye, the cloth looks like the dye, the cloth feels like the dye. This is what they called baptiso, which is the present day word baptism.

Similarly, Jesus Christ the Baptist also stands by the river of the spirit and fire and baptizes us into him.

> *As for me, I baptize you with water for repentance, but He who is coming after me is mightier than I, and I am not fit to remove His sandals; He will baptize you with the Holy Spirit and fire.*
>
> Matthew 3:11

He takes as many as come to him and immerses us fully into the Holy Ghost and fire and once we get the real Holy Ghost baptism we receive a 100% transformation of our nature, our entire being accepts the character and the nature of the Holy Spirit and we become like the Holy Spirit. We look spiritually like the Holy Spirit, we smell like the Holy Spirit, our entire personality will be soaked into the Holy Spirit and fire; spiritually we become one with the Holy Spirit.

Peter, John and the apostles, after they had received this Holy Spirit and fire baptism, received a transformation which was phenomenal. They did not only speak in tongues and shout, they saw a cripple and say *silver and gold have I none, but such as I have give I unto you, in the name of Jesus rise up and walk.* They healed the sick and delivered many oppressed and afflicted by demons. They became firebrands and were dripping fire everywhere they went. They were "hot" disciples of Christ, the gate of hell could not prevail against them, they were flames of fire which could not be quenched by authorities, principalities and powers.

Stage 5

Potter's Wheel Experience

**THE 5TH STAGE IS
THE FORMING OF THE VESSEL**

The word forming comes from the Hebrew word *Yatsar*, meaning to mold or to squeeze into shape as the potter does. Another word for form which is to make, comes from the word *panah*, which means to skilfully form.

Then the LORD God formed man of dust from the ground, and breathed into his nostrils the breath of life; and man became a living being.
Genesis 2:7

The creation of man is the greatest of all God's creation, which is why He created man in His own image and likeness and made him to rule and to dominate the earth. Let us analyze this man, the only creation that God made in his own image and likeness and also considered higher than angels. Men are formed, not from precious and rich minerals like gold and silver or diamonds, but from ordinary dust of the earth. Dust (clay) is from the Hebrew word *aphar*, meaning mud or rubbish. The forming stage can also be defined as developing man (clay, dust and rubbish) into a distinctive shape or figure that would be more valuable than silver, gold and diamonds and can never be purchased by them.

The Formation Stage

The formation stage is the most difficult of all the stages; it requires much time, undivided attention, art and skill. At this stage, the potter divides the clay into small piles. The clay is now ready to be wedged, which is a lot like kneading bread dough. The potter must push the clay down flat, pull it up and fold it over repeatedly to give the clay its elasticity. After being wedged, the clay is cut with a wire into correct sizes according to the kind of vessel that it will become. The potter then begins to shape each piece into round balls and sets them aside to age in an airtight container.

In the process of our being developed into vessels of honor and blessing, our transformation does not happen all of a sudden and our change can never be overnight. As the clay is divided into small pieces first of about three or four handfuls each before the potter starts his work of transformation, so it is with God, the master potter, who guides us through our changes step by step and little by little. God never works on all our attitudes and abilities overnight. His patience and longsuffering towards us while He works on us is incomparable and never comes to an end. They are new every morning. God is not a slave master so He never expects too much from us while He is working on us. All He requires from us is to be obedient and willing.

Dear reader, God does not start anything from the middle, neither does He continues anybody's project. His processes are simple, He starts it Himself and ends it Himself; that is why He is the Alpha and the Omega. First, he will put us down flat and knead us like dough, which is to ensure that any air or bubbles (self and pride) that have gotten into us and are inflating us to look big in our own eyes and also in the eyes of people are well removed from within. This is what he did to Moses in the land of the Midianites, in the wilderness after he fled from Egypt. He then stretches us till our skin becomes elastic; we become impenetrable by outside element and factors, which means that, no matter what people will do against us and the factors that will be against us, we will still not be emotional and give in. Beloved, before God certifies us to be His generals, He will make us go through series of painful spiritual exercises without any considerations aimed at eliminating emotions and weaknesses from us. We cannot be frontliners for God if we are emotional and weak. If God does not eliminate these two insidious factors from us, they have the potential to eliminate us before we fulfill our mission on earth for God.

Most athletes understand that in order for them to be great in their craft, there will be stretching involved that will challenge them to their next level. This concept is also true for God's children. Whenever

God desires to stretch His children to the next level, He is always going to challenge us.
In order for the greatness that is sitting deep inside of us to come alive, we must accept the challenge and allow the stretch to begin. God is always stretching us to become better people.

On the Potter's Wheel

One day, the prophet Jeremiah was asked by the Lord to visit the local potter's house. Being obedient and also being puzzled, he went. As he drew near the potter's house which served as a workshop, too, he watched the potter take a piece of clay from the mass that lay beside him and knead it to get rid of its bubbles. Then he shaped the clay into a round ball and set it aside to age in an airtight container. The potter then placed the clay on the potter's wheel as a round blob; the clay was formed into a specific, useful shape on the potter's wheel. One trademark of a master potter is a loud thud as the round ball of clay is slammed onto the spinning potter's wheel close to the center. This technique alone takes great skill. At this point the clay ball will be spinning around in the middle of the wheel, but it is still a little wobbly and no other work can be done until it is perfectly centered on the wheel. This is accomplished by the robust immovable grip of the potter's hand pressing into it on both sides. The clay has no other choice but to be conformed into a perfectly centered ball of clay. The potter then releases his hand slowly because of the tremendous amount of force being exerted on the clay. If his hands are removed too quickly, the clay is worse off than when the process first began.

The potter then plunges his thumb down the middle of the clay ball to form the initial opening of the vessel. His hand squeezes in from the bottom and starts to pull up slowly so that the vessel begins to grow in height. A master potter needs only three good pulls to bring the vessel to its final height and thickness. During those three pulls, the potter's hands are able to determine what kind of vessel it will become, based on the elasticity and eagerness of the clay.

What starts off as a piece of mud clay may end up as a durable and valuable vessel, which will be sought after by kings and royals and used in the royal palaces. This is because the potter realizes the capability of the clay to stand and take shape as it is being formed. If the molding is not in agreement with the intended shape, it is sometimes squished down, scraped off and tossed back into the wet clay barrel for formation to be done later. However, if the potter is happy with the overall shape of the vessel, it then stays so. Any design or patterns seen on vessels are made at this time while the vessel is still soft and pliable.

The potter's wheel is a machine that rapidly revolves horizontally at the motion of the foot driving the treadle. The potter's wheel is actually made up of two wheels. A large one is suspended above a hole in the floor connected to an upright wheel. Using the feet, the potter turns the lower wheel which causes movement through the pole resulting in the turning of the upper wheel.

Spinning Stage

Spinning is an ancient textile art in which fibres are converted into yarns or thread. It is an act of being rotated very fast. In the potter's house, the potter at this stage takes the prepared clay and then violently strikes it on the spinning potter's wheel which produces an unpleasant sound and then keeps it right in the center of the spinning wheel while the immovable robust grip of the potter's hand is pressing hard into it on both sides.

Dear reader, this act of the potter towards the clay at this stage seems so unpleasant, unfriendly and very rough. It is in the same manner God treats and handles us whenever we are just about to be molded. He picks us up and then slams us on the potter's spinning wheel; this act of God at this stage of life brings physical pains and discomfort to us.

At this time we feel so lonely, not loved and hated. It seems like God does not care about what we are going through and He has not even seen it. At such times, because of the pain and the discomfort that we are going through we begin to ask questions like, is God really there? Has He called me? Am I in the right place and ministry? Am I in His perfect or permissive will? Is He really with me? Sometimes our minds become full of 101 questions without immediate answers. It is this stage that Abram got to when God told him at the age of over 100 years to journey for days to a mountain and then sacrifice his only son of promise, Isaac. It is at this stage also that the Israelites got to in the days of Gideon when they were being oppressed by the Midianites and Gideon asked the angel, if the Lord is with us why are we going through all this? It is at this stage that Christ our Lord got to when the scriptures called him a man of sorrow and acquainted with grief. He was despised, betrayed, rejected, batted, bruised, beaten and wounded by his own and yet he never said a word. It was the night that his sweat was like blood and he cried, *Father if it is your will take this cup from me*, it was this stage that the Christians of old got to when they were brought before the tyrant's throne and flogged, tortured, imprisoned. Some were even put into the lion's den and killed.

This is what made Jesus tell his disciples that a servant is not greater than his master. It is the stage of persecution and testing of faith. It is the time that, if care is not taken, one will give up the faith and question the very existence of God and doubt his calling.

Dear reader, for the clay to be in the center of the spinning wheel, the potter has to put it there. The potter does not leave the clay while it is on the wheel. It is said and believed that the only time the clay experiences the robust, immovable, strong grip of the both the potter's hands is when the potter's wheel is on high speed and the clay is sitting right in the center. Anything apart from a strong, immovable grip of the potter's hands on the clay, will make the clay fly off. It is also believed that the only time that the potter does not shift his focus and attention, not even for a split second, from the clay is once again as it sits on the wheel and it is being shaped or molded. Again, it is believed that while the clay is on the spinning wheel, if the potter shifts his focus or attention for just a split second he will not have the type of shape he intends.

Brother and Sister in Christ, it is the same with God and us, when we go through our period of trials and persecution (testing of our faith) God must allow it, for He knows our strength, and will not allow us to be tested above what we can afford. For the trials and test come not to destroy us, but to toughen us and shape us. God will not leave us alone in our period of trials and testing.

> *When you pass through the waters, I will be with you; And through the rivers, they will not overflow you. When you walk through the fire, you will not be scorched, Nor will the flame burn you.*
>
> Isaiah 43:2

Dear Colleague, like the potter and the clay, the Lord knows that our strength is but little and that we are weak, so the times that our faith is seriously challenged, the Lord knows that our only saving grace will be the sufficiency of His grace and his own strength for us. As he told Paul in 2 Corinthians 12:9-10, in the times that we think He has left us and that we feel so lonely, weak and abandoned, this is the very time He shows himself so strong like a pillar of cloud by day and the pillar of fire by night, and promises that He will never leave us nor forsake us and that He will be with us until the very end. God knows that in our time of trials, tests and weaknesses, if He does not show Himself strong, we will not be able to survive because that trial has the potential of shaking us from Him and then we will be headed for a crush, as the spinning wheel throws off any loose clay. So He holds us up and on with His mighty hands. The times that we think that the dark clouds have covered us so much that He does not see what we are going through, it is that very time that He fixes his eyes on every detail of our lives.

> *The eyes of the LORD are toward the righteous And His ears are open to their cry. The face of the LORD is against evildoers, To cut off the memory of them from the earth. The righteous cry, and the LORD hears And delivers them out of all their troubles. The LORD is near to the broken hearted And saves those who are crushed in spirit. Many are the afflictions of the righteous, But the LORD delivers him out of them all. He keeps all his bones, Not one of them is broken. Evil shall slay the wicked, And those who hate the righteous will be condemned. The LORD redeems the soul of His servants, And none of those who take refuge in Him will be condemned.*
>
> Psalm34:15-22

There is one trademark of every good potter as he is works on the clay; it is the sound of a loud thud as he slams the ball of clay onto the spinning potter's wheel to mold it. The sound of the loud thud is so unpleasant, people who are outside the potter's house always wonder what is happening.

It is the same when the Lord slams us on the wheels (trials and tests). The sound which is produced is so unpleasant; we hear reports and news that are bone breaking, we are falsely accused on every side, there are lot of rumors and lies and allegations about us, we are called names, we are heavily criticized by the media and are put on headlines and breaking news and so forth and so on. Jesus warned *woe unto us if all men speak well of us.*

It is a known fact in pottery that, in order for the ball of clay to be molded as a vessel, it should be perfectly centered right in the middle of the spinning wheel. If not it cannot be worked on. In the same manner, God places us right in the center of trials and tests. Not the edges, but in the middle where we cannot just jump out but when we have survived the trials, we will be able to tell others where our makings and greatness started and strengthen our fellow brethren, and encourage them that we have been through it before and tell them it will be well. It is not meant to destroy but make us up. We should see those trials and tests as stepping stones into greatness and not as obstacles.

Each scandal, attack, allegation, rumor or lie about us is an opportunity for us to be well known and be well broadcasted. For if your enemies know that by being instrument of lies and attacks, our families and ministries will be catapulted into fame, success and achievement, they will advise themselves. The Bible says if the prince of this world would have known he would not have crucified the Christ, because just that act of crucifying Christ has brought disarmament, destructions, made public spectacles of them while bringing salvation to the whole world and restoring man back to God. Dear reader, let me upset your philosophy now. Sometimes God works hand in hand with your enemies, God allows your enemies to finish their worst then He, God, begins His best for you. All God will be saying to us is *be still and know that I am God.*

It is also a known fact that the clay is kept on the fast spinning wheel by the immovable grips of the potter's hands, and that if his hands are removed too quickly the clay becomes worse off than when the process first began. Beloved, what has kept us alive and not shattered in the mist of all our troubles, trials and tests is simply the immovable hands of God upon our lives. It is not our might nor by our strength but just the saving hands. It is His hands that keep us faithful and still abiding in Him.

Shaping Up

To shape up means to develop or to improve so as to meet a standard. During this stage the potter releases his grip on the clay on the spinning wheel very slowly because of the tremendous amount of force being applied or exerted on the clay.

So far as God is our potter and is transforming us to be vessels of honor in His court, after He has kneaded us and stretched us, He will put us on the wheels. The potter's wheel is one of the most uncomfortable places in the potter's house, and it is the very place where God molds His vessels.

From the moment the potter's hands are at work with the clay on the wheel, the potter will mold the clay from within and without, shaping up with his fingers the vessel which may be used for the temple court or the royal palace.

The process of molding and shaping the clay might seem obscure and very rough but that is the best method to have a great vessel made. While the clay is being spun, the potter's hands will be molding and shaping it up.

When the potter starts working on a new project, he starts with a lump of clay, and not with a finished product. It's just mud clay which goes through a series of changes and transformations to be shaped into a vessel which becomes fit to be used in the court of God's temple or the king's royal palace.

There is a song we like singing very much. It goes like this: *Change my heart, oh God, make it ever true, change my heart, oh God, and may I be like you. You are the potter and I am clay, mold me and make me, this is what I pray.* The question is, do we really sing this song honestly? Most of us love what we are and we would not change it for any kind of life, but God sees us as a ball of clay on the potter's wheel, not even close to the shape He intends for us and never close to being useful. He sees us as raw and unfinished products and yet we are so pleased with ourselves.

The only process we need to go through in order for us to be shaped up for the purpose he intends for us is called change. Change remains inevitable not just because time moves on, and not just because everything is becoming obsolete, but simply because God is at work. So far us we are on the potter's wheel and the potter's fingers are shaping us, we will go through the processes of change.

Surprisingly, the only person who wants change is a wet baby. We all want the glory but do not want to endure the cross; we want to be great and yet still we do not want to pay the price. And how we would like to be in heaven but never want to die. For a piece of clay to be transformed to a vessel fit for use in the court of God's temple or the king's palace it has to go through painful transitional changes, unless we want to remain as we are. The only one who does not need change is God, because only God is perfect, whole and finished. The rest of us are all a work in progress.

Beloved, let us just look at this for a moment: It is not pastors, apostles or leaders who try to shape us or try to change us, but God. God uses both good forces and forces of the enemy to change us. Whenever the need arose, He used the enemies of Israel, the Babylonian forces, to shape up Israel into the vessel He wanted it to be. The Babylonians who were used in punishing the Israelites were not good guys, but God still allowed them to press the Israelites hard on every side.

> *And we know that God causes all things to work together for good to those who love God, to those who are called according to His purpose.*
> *Romans 8:28*

Squeezing Out Into Shape

At this stage on the potter's wheel, the potter's hands squeeze in on the clay from the bottom. To squeeze out in pottery means to press or to force out into shape. The squeezing and the pressing gives to the vessel a unique shape that attracts potential buyers and users. It also adds style and value to the vessel making it look more like an artistic vessel of beauty and wonder.

It is a known fact that straight-figured vessels are not costly. I mean they are very cheap and can be purchased at any price in the market, but the vessels which are artistically designed with curves which come as a result of squeezing and bending are very expensive. Sometimes in an auction, their prices get into millions of American dollars and British pounds. They are the very vessels that are used to decorate the temple court and the royal palaces, not the straight-figured ones.

The easily made straight-figured vessels do not require any special skill in their making. They get on the potters' wheels and in just minutes they are made, but the architecturally designed vessels which are made through bending curves, squeezing and pressures come from hard pressings requiring specially trained professionals with years of experience and skills. It takes a longer time for such a vessel to be made; they are never made in an instant.

The squeezing and the pressing into shape are not comfortable at all; they come with excruciating pains, pressures and restlessness but the reward is priceless– a second-to-none vessel, vessels without any competitor, highly expensive vessels and vessels made for honorable purposes.

Dear reader, all vessels that the Lord molds for honorable and great purposes go through squeezing and the pressing times. The pains that we experience, and the circumstances we are faced with are the fingers of the potter's hands pressing us into the God kind of shape, and making us into vessels God wants us to be. Some things that we think are going to destroy us at those times turn out to be God's hand taking a misshapen vessel and collapsing it into a lump of clay so He can start all over again. The truth is that we would never have changed had it not been for the pressure and pain we experience. We would never have grown up or learned to depend on God if that thing we consider bad never happened.

Some of us know we are that marred pots on the wheel, and that we are good for nothing, but we see the hand of God coming in to squeeze and press us out into shape and we cry, oh no! We can't survive it. No, God is not going to destroy us; rather, He is shaping and molding us for His own glory and for His own name's sake. Sometimes God allows the ordeals and storms of life to come to us, not because He is venting His anger at us, but it is all about reshaping us for his purpose.

Wisdom tells us God is able to use all the circumstances throughout our lives to shape us. Even when the bad things happen to us, God is able to work them together for our good. We can see that some cruelty, sicknesses and losses endured produced some kind of good in the end. We can say as Joseph said to his brothers, you intended it for evil, but God intended it for good.

> *"Now do not be grieved or angry with yourselves, because you sold me here, for God sent me before you to preserve life.*
> *Genesis 45:5*

The problem is that we are all farsighted. We can see it at a distance and the truth is that God is at work in all our circumstances, as we are being shaped. Paul the apostle puts it beautifully in 2 Corinthians 4:7, but we have this treasure in earthen vessels, so that the surpassing greatness of the power will be of God and not from ourselves. And just a few verses later, though, he said we have this treasure in jars of clay, he said this is how that sharpening looks like in his life.

We are afflicted in every way, but not crushed; perplexed, but not despairing; persecuted, but not forsaken; struck down, but not destroyed;
2 Corinthians 4:8,9

Throughout the process we are being transformed. We are being shaped into vessels for His use. After the potter's hand squeezes the clay from the bottom, he starts to pull up the vessel slowly so that the vessel begins to increase in height and thickness. So it is with us and God: It is in our unusual trials and tests that God blesses us with increase in growth. Dear friend, anything that is of God increases and expands under pressure.
Joseph died, and all his brothers, and all that generation. But the sons of Israel were fruitful and increased greatly, and multiplied, and became exceedingly mighty, so that the land was filled with them. Now a new king arose over Egypt, who did not know Joseph. He said to his people,

> *"Behold, the people of the sons of Israel are more and mightier than we. Come, let us deal wisely with them, or else they will multiply and in the event of war, they will also join themselves to those who hate us, and fight against us and depart from the land." So they appointed taskmasters over them to afflict them with hard labor. And they built for Pharaoh storage cities, Pithom and Raamses. But the more they afflicted them, the more they multiplied and the more they spread out, so that they were in dread of the sons of Israel.*
>
> Exodus 1: 6-12

Verse 12 is my favourite; the more they afflicted them the more they multiplied and grew. I like this, beloved. It is a known fact that persecution and trials have always caused the church to grow. In the book of Acts the more the disciples were being mocked, beaten, imprisoned and killed, the more they increased and multiplied. This is the true sign of every true child of God; we don't perish and crush in times of trials, tests and persecutions. It is an unwritten law that persecution, tests and trials only strengthen and toughen the people of God and the Church and afflicted people always find ways and means to resist until they are strong enough to overcome their oppressors or the enemies.

During the pulling up by the gentle hands of the potter to determine the thickness and the height of the vessel, the potter is able to determine what kind of vessel it will be, based on its elasticity and eagerness. Dear reader, the process of our growth and greatness does not come cheap, spinning on the wheel, the squeezing into shape, the pull ups, are all with pains and agony which we must yield fully to and trust God. As the clay on the wheel being shaped, squeezed and being pulled up can not say to the potter, get off, that hurts, but stays there to be fashioned according to the plan and purpose of the potter, so we human beings, although not exactly like clay, of course, have the right to get off the wheel, even though that might mean our being spattered all over the place! If God is to make us to become the vessel of honor to serve his purposes on earth fully, then we have be eager and yield to God and the finger of the Holy Spirit in the same way that the clay responds to the gentle hands of the potter.

We have to trust that the experience we have which makes and fashions us will be for our own good. We have to trust that God will use our ordeals, our ordinariness and the humdrumness of our lives to make us into beautiful and attractive vessels of honor.

What started off as an unworthy lump of clay may end up as a vessel that the potter will take pride in and that will give him joy; he will then start his finishing touches by putting any designs and patterns on it while the clay is still soft and pliable.

Stage 6

Shelving, Cabinet or Waiting Period

THE 6TH STAGE IS CALLED THE SHELVING AND CABINET PERIOD

The new, still soft vessel is now put aside in a special cabinet to dry slowly along with other vessels in the same condition. Just a little bit of air is allowed to flow into the cabinet to even out the moisture. If the vessel dries too quickly it will crack, and too much effort has been put into it at this stage for that to happen. Therefore it is closely monitored for slow and even drying. When the vessel has dried enough to resemble leather, it is removed from the cabinet. It is then put back on the potter's wheel, upside down this time, so that it rough edges can be trimmed. Now it will sit in the open air until it is completely dry.

The cabinet is an upright cupboard like a repository with shelves, drawers or compartments for the safekeeping or display of vessels. It can also be termed as a closet and the term shelving means to hold back or postpone.

Dear Colleague, the shelving and the cabinet period is so essential for the potter and the vessel;

it is not this stage that the potter can afford to avoid. It is the stage that the vessel has been freshly and fully made and is looking so promising and so well. At this stage, the vessel is now all that it will be in shape and function, but it is not yet ready to be used. It is brittle and any rough handling or moisture will ruin it.

Beloved, it is the same way God deals with the vessels he has made to serve his purpose. God does not expose the vessels he has made prematurely; he keeps us in his closet so we mature slowly. God allows just a little bit of air around us at this stage. This is to say that God does not make us public nor broadcast us nor makes us feel special or important; neither does he give us the freedom to move around. He does give us some airs, but He allows just a small flow around us because too much of it can ruin our gift and callings before our time of exposure arrives.

These are the times that we can be become vulnerable to the spirit of delusion, we can be deceived into thinking we have it all, and that we are even more gifted than our fathers who took us from ghettos and mentored us until now—because at this stage we are fresh, and newly made. We may appear to be even stronger than our fathers, but that is a lie! It might look like we are preferred to our fathers but it is also a lie from the camp of familiar spirit. It was a lie when the women of Israel in 1 Samuel 18:7 sang, *Saul has slain his thousands but David his ten thousands.*

This is the stage because of some calling and gift we might have, if we become loose, the enemies of progress who might be our fellow brothers and sisters might urge us to rebel against authorities and the fathers by praising and flattering us with all sorts of lies and jargons or illusions and makes us feel important and big. If we are not spiritually wise, we will find 101 faults with our fathers and begin to fight them and then break away from our father's house, thinking we can start our own and make it bigger than our father's. Folks, it is all right to leave our father's house when the time is due, but it is all wrong to break out from our father's house. We would never leave with their blessings and we can be cursed and crushed.

The fact that we have the calling does not mean that we have been called to be on the front line, believe me. It is not all soldiers who fight on the front lines. Those who offer themselves to fight on the front lines get a stray bullet and become disabled or die foolishly.

Waiting

Our saving grace in the cabinet and on the potter's shelf is waiting. During the time that we wait for our appointed time to mature, although it might seem like we have the ability to function and perform in the areas we have been made for, we might not be used for that purpose. Instead, we may be used for different things altogether which might not have any correlation to our God-given assignment. For example, Jesus Christ before his appointed time at the age of 30, was called the carpenter's son. Folks, carpentry has no link to saving the world but that is what he spent most of his time doing before his appointed time arrived.

Another example I will give is Moses. For the first 40 years of his life, he was in the pharaoh's palace, and the second 40 years of his life he was a shepherd in a strange land and also serving Jethro his father-in-law. It was just the last 40 years of his life that his real call started unfolding. Looking at David, prior to his being a king, he was in the shepherd bush and actively engaged in killing lions and bears. Elisha, until he received Elijah's mantle, was plowing with his father's camel. Gideon was pressing wheat when the Lord called him. Paul after his conversion did not become an apostle immediately. He was serving and making tents till his gifting and calling unfolded. Even in the army you will find soldiers who do all kinds of trades. Meanwhile, their main purpose is to defend and fight.

Folks, no one might dispute the fact that we have been called to reach the world and bring revival to nations, etc., but some of the times our fathers would make us do something entirely different in the church. For example, we might be called upon to play drums, usher, lead opening and closing prayer, pray over the offering, count money like Philip the Evangelist, or clean and arrange chairs for some period of time. Meanwhile, we know it has nothing to do with our callings and sometimes some of us get offended and begin to accuse our fathers of refusing to recognize our gift in the church. Sometimes some of us even think the fathers are being political. This is where most of us kill our callings and gifting before we even get started. In most of the cases, it is not the immorality factor that kills, but the lack of submission factor that kills young gift and anointing before they become public.

Potter's School of Wilderness

Rod Nash, a wilderness historian, said that wilderness is a difficult word to define. While the word is a noun, it acts like an adjective. There is no specific material or object that is a wilderness. Rod Nash said "There is no universal definition of wilderness." He also believes that wilderness is so heavily weighed with meaning of a personal, symbolic and changing kind that it makes it is difficult to define.

It is said in early Teutonic and Norse languages from which the English language developed, the root word, "will" meant "self-willed," wilful or uncontrollable. The adjective "willed" is used to convey the idea of being lost, unruly, disordered or confused. Applied initially to human conduct, the term was extended to wildlife or wild animals "as being out of control of a man." Other Europeans define wilderness as a deserted place, a place lacking cultivation. Wilderness is conceived as a region where a person is likely to get into a disordered, confused or wild condition.

Even in today's dictionaries, wilderness is defined as uncultivated, in other words, undeveloped land. The absence of men or a non-human environment is a common modern day perception. The usual dictionary meaning of wilderness implies hostility on man's part.

The word wilderness used on man's part is an idiomatic expression meaning that one has found himself in an inhospitable, alien, life-threatening condition within a period of time. Wilderness is not the final destination for the servant of God, but it is the place God leads us through. One would ask the question: why is that God does not use us right away but leads us through the wilderness before he uses us to fulfill his purpose on earth? The answer is simple. Firstly, he does that in order to humble us, secondly, to see the type of heart we have, thirdly to grow and cause us to be mature.

Consider it all joy, my brethren, when you encounter various trials, knowing that the testing of your faith produces endurance. And let endurance have its perfect result, so that you may be perfect and complete, lacking in nothing.
James 1:2-4

Wilderness school experience may seem unbearable to those who are in it, but you can be confident that God will not lead us into something with the intention to destroy us. For God knows that there are short cuts but dangerous routes to our promised land. For example, God could have led the Israelite to Canaan through a shorter route, but that could have made them return to Egypt and the plans of God would not be fulfilled (Exodus 13:17-18).

The wilderness school should not be a self-sent one; God would have to lead us to and through it. Self-sent wilderness experience can get us killed or can lead us to abandon the faith, but when the spirit leads us to it, we can be confident that whatever we will be going through can be overcome.

Our attitude and response to the trials and tests determine our duration in the wilderness. For example in our natural academic and professional world today, some individuals start a professional course and they never get finished. Some start it and in just two and a half years they are finished. Meanwhile, some spend over ten years before they complete. This is due to our attitudes and how we conduct ourselves when faced with those tests.

The Bible frequently uses the Old Testament nation of Israel as a symbol of Christians today. As they were slaves in Egypt, so are we slaves to sin. It was not the will of God to take them through the wilderness for those 40 years, but their selfish attitudes prolonged their days in the wilderness. In their trials, instead of thanking God, they complained and they grumbled. Instead of acknowledging that God was in control of their entire lives and even the trials, they became bitter. They allowed the suffering to take hold of them and then eat into them like cancer until that generation died in the wilderness. Instead of taking refuge in God and not allowing the suffering to get to them, they remained impatient in their wilderness and did not reverence the Lord. Instead of reverently pouring out their heart to the Lord and waiting patiently for his strength and provision, they murmured. The rebels who were among them had greedy desires; and also the sons of Israel wept again and said, "Who will give us meat to eat? We remember the fish which we used to eat free in Egypt, the cucumbers and the melons and the leeks and the onions and the garlic, but now our appetite is gone. There is nothing at all to look at except this manna." Numbers 11:4-6

If only we could learn to wait on the Lord patiently and then praise him wherever and whenever we are faced with difficulties, the Lord will provide the strength and our wilderness journey will not be long but will be over soon.

As children of God, we should learn to prove our loyalty to God and his word during our time in the wilderness like Jesus Christ did. If only we will learn to tell the devil "it is written," in the presence of nobody or when no one is watching us in our wilderness, when we come to the public, he would be the first to shout out to the hearing of the many, that I know you, you are the son of God and have you come to torment us before our time. Even the devils and the demons will respect you because you did not bow nor give in to them when no one was watching you, but if we lose our integrity and bow to the devil in the presence of no one and mess up, when we become public he will disgrace us in the presence of all. The devil will tell us Jesus I know and Paul I know but who are you? If we lose it during our wilderness days, we cannot prove it when we become public, for that would be termed as hypocrisy in the eyes of God, men and the devil, and we can never be used by God to build up and edify the church and to save the dying world with the grace he has given to us.

Wilderness also means the place outside our comfort zone. *Comfortable circumstances are what most people want, if not all of us, because in comfort you can pursue things that are familiar to you and also it makes life far easier. However comfort is death to achievement and creativity. It can destroy potential. It can neutralize the force called multiplication and increase. In life it is believed comfortable people achieve little.* Comfort zones may come in the form of cushy jobs, comfy lifestyles or a very smooth and successful career path. In his book, *The Journey Beyond the Comfort Zone,* by David W. F. Wong, Dr John Edmond Haggai, who is the founder and the chairman of Haggai Institute said in his forward that "comfort cannot give us the spur to achieve, difficulties and hardships can." He also said that, "In any field of human endeavour it is those who pay the price for excellence who come out to the top."

You can bear me out that almost all the life-changing experience of the heroes of our faith, took place outside of the comfort zone.

The first is about the conception, the birth and the life of Jesus Christ, which is the greatest ever life-changing event at all time. It took place outside his place of comfort. I see it as a glorious defining moment, because it changed the course of human life, directed our path to life and glory, defined it and then gave it meaning.

Jesus the Christ was conceived when his mother Mary was still a virgin, but how could she explain this to anyone and be justified. It might be termed simply as madness on the part of Mary and Joseph because it does not make sense biologically, logically and philosophically. I'm quite sure this was an embarrassment and a shame to Mary, Joseph, both families and also the baby Jesus. This is one of the greatest discomforts that anybody can ever experience, but God chose that means to let his only begotten son come to the world to become our Savior. Is it not stupendous!

As though that experience was not enough, Jesus the King of Kings, the only begotten of the father, the Savior of the world, was not born in the king's palace or a royal hospital, not even in an a ordinary home, but he was born in one of the most uncomfortable environments, a place no woman would ever choose to have her first baby, a manger in Bethlehem, because there was no room for them in the inn.

In addition, throughout the life changing ministry of our Lord Jesus Christ on earth, preaching the good news to the poor; healing the broken hearted; preaching deliverance to the captive; recovering of sight to the blind and setting at liberty them that are bruised, he was able to work these works of God in a hostile and difficult environment.

> *And Jesus said to him, "The foxes have holes and the birds of the air have nests, but the Son of Man has nowhere to lay His head."*
> Luke 9:58

Also, the greatest event that has ever taken place in the world that shook the heavens, the earth and the foundations of hell, the devil and his kingdom, which brought about the greatest deliverance and the total liberation of the creation and humanity, took place on the cross. There the King of Kings and the Lord of Lords became ordinary flesh and was humiliated, a spectacle to the whole world. Jesus Christ was battered, bruised, and bled through beating, but he endured all to redeem and purchase us back to God. He had to go down, very far below his place of majesty and comfort.

Child of God, all the heroes of our faith who achieved glorious moments and made a name while serving God on earth, at one time God had to disrupt their routine comfy lifestyle and then yank them out of their places of comfort to achieve that excellent status and the blessings we all talk about today. The fact is that no one can be used greatly of God to save the dying world and build up the people of God if the person has not paid any price, and you know that price comes with pain.

God had to get father Abram from his country, his kindred and from his father's house to a strange land before he blessed him and made him a great nation and made him a blessing.

Joseph was hated by his own brothers, put in a pit, sold, accused falsely and imprisoned before he attained the highest position in Egypt after Pharaoh, the first foreign Egyptian prime minister.

God had to disturb the comfort of Moses by taking him from the king's palace and making him suffer affliction with the children of Israel and later on he was driven to the wilderness for 40 years and there he was made greatest leader of all time.

Apostle Paul was in chains most of the times he was writing almost half of the New Testament books.

John the apostle wrote the book of Revelation in the Island of Patmos.

Extraordinary Champions

It is uncomfortable people who produce miraculous changes in every generation. It is uncomfortable people who create the currents that change the very world we live in. Beloved, every extraordinary, superachiever in our world today and also, in the past, secured that greatness by going out of their comfort zones. Most of them made geographical changes that birthed their entry into this world's hall of fame of great superachievers. For example, in the Bible Ruth was willing to relocate geographically, she was willing to disconnect from her kinfolks and she was willing to go in a direction she had never been, to experience discomfort and the forfeiting of the ease of old friendships in order to birth one of the greatest chapters in history.

Moses

Let us analyze the character Moses. The name Moses means to draw out. He is the symbol of the prophets and the greatest leader of all time. However, he was born into slavery, and was not supposed to live. His name was given to him by his adopted mother, who was pharaoh's daughter who took him up and nourished him as her own son. Moses, in the first 40 years of his life, grew up in comfort and in luxury as a prince of Egypt and also as an army commander who led in conquering the enemies of Egypt. The scriptures say that he learned all the wisdom of the Egyptians and was mighty in words and in deeds and refused to be called the son of pharaoh's daughter but chose to suffer affliction with his brethren rather than to enjoy the pleasure of sin for a moment. Although he had the calling to deliver the children of Israel from slavery, he did not understand the divine timing, so he jumped out at that particular time to fulfill the calling and the mission and so failed the very people that he was assigned and called to protect. They even refused him because it was not yet time.

> *And he supposed that his brethren understood that God was granting them deliverance through him, but they did not understand. On the following day he appeared to them as they were fighting together, and he tried to reconcile them in peace, saying, "Men, you are brethren, why do you injure one another?" But the one who was injuring his neighbour pushed him away, saying, "WHO MADE YOU A RULER AND JUDGE OVER US? YOU DO NOT MEAN TO KILL ME AS YOU KILLED THE EGYPTIAN YESTERDAY, DO YOU?"*
> Acts 7:25-28

Had it not been that he fled to the wilderness, Pharaoh would have killed him before he even started fulfilling his calling and mission (Exodus 2:15).

Beloved, the experience of Moses at that stage is a lesson to be learned by all of us who are young but have the genuine calling and the grace. As Moses deceived himself, thinking that his own people would understand that God was using him to save them, so he had to start something in line with his calling and he ended up almost being killed. It is the same for some of us who have the grace and the calling and are being prepared for a particular work. The temptation that we can be deceived like Moses to start it before the appointed time is so great. Our inability to know the right time to start what we are being prepared to do in the future for God has resulted in spiritual abortion of potential gifts and callings that could have been used for greater works in these end times.

Aggression and impatience have ended many genuinely gifted and called individuals. The very moment we act before God's appointed time we become vulnerable, we make mistakes that might not be forgiven and we expose ourselves to problems and hardships that can break and destroy us. Being called but sending yourself before you are sent is equivalent to not being called, but remember God does not sponsor and support anybody's vision and project but he sponsors and supports the vision and project he has given to men to achieve on earth.

And in the next 40 years of his life, Moses was forced into the wilderness where he was shaped and grew as a deliverer. The wilderness school was indispensable in the making of Moses as the world's greatest leader and deliverer; it is where his real training as a leader and a deliverer began.

Moses had servants who served him in Egypt, but in the wilderness school, his first lesson was to learn to serve by being a servant. God took Egypt out of him and made him an ordinary man. He was actually described as an Egyptian in Exodus 2:18-19.

God took Moses from the place of his pride and self to the wilderness to humble him so that he would learn to abide and walk with him in order to work his purpose and plans through him, for he hates a proud attitude (Deuteronomy 8:2, James 4:6, Isaiah 57:15).

The secret of abiding and walking with God is the key for being a useful vessel for God. In that 40 years in the wilderness, Moses was tested and tried by the Lord in order for the content of his heart to be revealed, before he would send him out to fulfill his God-given assignment. The wilderness tests and trials are so important to God, even in the life of Jesus Christ. Before he could begin fulfilling his assignment on earth, the spirit led him to the wilderness to be tested.

The wilderness school should not be a self-sent one; you have to be led by the Lord to the wilderness school. In the wilderness school, it is only God, you and the devil who will be there, no one else. If you send yourself to the wilderness school, you will pay for it painfully and you might not come back alive. It is where God allows the enemy to bring temptations and trials of all kinds, it is where we really feel the absence of God with our five senses, but it is also where God is actually present.

Absalom

Absalom was the third son of King David. The Bible describes him in 2 Samuel 14:25 as being beautiful. Absalom was graced with beauty but he was deceitful, demanding and a smooth talker who desired to be king of Israel. Since he was the third in line to succeed King David, it did not look so promising for him to become the king of Israel, so he launched into a revolt against David to take over the throne. Absalom had always had his eyes on his father's throne.

> *In this manner Absalom dealt with all Israel who came to the king for judgment; so Absalom stole away the hearts of the men of Israel.*
> 2 Samuel 15:6

The gift and the grace that Absalom had made him steal the hearts of his father's men, and later on he declared himself a king and left his father David running for his life. Unfortunately, Absalom had no right to win the heart of his father's men. That is why the Bible uses the phrase "he stole." As we all know, we need people in order to be king and without the people there cannot be a king, so for Absalom to steal the hearts of the people from his father because of his gift and grace was a very dangerous thing. Later on, the very gift and the grace he was blessed with trapped and killed him, because he did not use it correctly.

Dear reader, Absaloms are always around. They are the graced and the gifted young individuals. Unfortunately, it is the graced and most gifted people who are tempted to become the Absaloms of today. With the grace, the gift and the anointing, we attract all kinds of people and their praises, but that should not make us rebel against our superiors and our fathers, thinking we are one with them or the same as they are and then fighting them at times.

When the gift and the grace we have been blessed with are not rightly and appropriately used, what was given to us to be blessings to us and to others will later on be a curse, a snare and the same gift and grace will kill us.

The Potter's Highway Experience

A highway is a main road for fast moving traffic, having different exits, limited access and separate lanes for vehicles travelling in the opposite direction. It is always a risk to take it whenever anyone is using it, because both good and bad drivers use it. Different people use it for different purposes and for different destinations. Some use the fast lane and others do not use the fast lane. Depending on the time of using the highway and your destination, some might come across free flowing traffic and others might come across heavily congested traffic. Different exits lead to different destinations, and once you know where you are going, the exit onto which you turn matters. For some of the exits, once you make a mistake and turn onto it, your only way back to the highway again is to go back to where you started the journey from, while some of the exits would take you in the opposite direction to your actual destination. In other words, it not every exit you see or come across that you can turn onto. Whenever there is an accident on the highway, or diversion or any form of danger on the highway, on some of the highways we have a highway escort who leads and directs vehicles to the right and safe route. Some vehicles do get themselves involved in heavy accidents which do result, in some cases, in loss of lives and the vehicles becoming obsolete or useless are sent to the scrap yard. In some cases also the driver becomes disabled for the rest of his life and his vehicle is damaged beyond repair, all because they did not follow instructions and did not follow the escort provided to lead.

Ministry is likened to a vehicle and the highway likened to the road that leads to the fulfillment of the calling and the assignment. The road that leads to the fulfilling of our God-given assignment is not a straight one and it is always a risk taken whenever anyone is journeying on it. Accidents do occur on that road. It is not a road we can be careless on, it is a road requiring that all of our five senses should be active at every point in time. It is a road of total vigilance because a slight mistake can be fatal to you and also affect many who are also traveling on it. It is a road where every regulation and rule must seriously and tenaciously be adhered to. Becoming loose and unprofessional on it for just a second can cost us so much that we might not be able to recover fully for the rest of our lives.

Jesus gave the parable of the Good Samaritan in the book of Luke 10:30 about a certain man who went down from Jerusalem to Jericho and fell among thieves and robbers. The ministry route is not only used by individuals with genuine callings and gifts but also some individuals who are wolves in sheepskin. As some people use the highway with the intention of causing accidents, to rob, and some also to commit suicide, so it is the same with some individuals who only come to the ministry to kill other ministries and gifts while others enter it to satisfy their selfish purposes. The road that leads from Jerusalem to Jericho is the same road from Jericho to Jerusalem. The same gifts and callings that build and edify people are used sometimes to destroy and ruin others. You know, the line that divides true and false gifts is so thin it requires the gift of discernment to be able to distinguish the wolves in the sheepskin from the real sheep.

The Lord knows that the road that leads to fulfilling his purposes on earth is quite dangerous, and that some gifts and callings get killed just before they get started or halfway through. Because of that he provides aids in order to ensure our safety, but in the midst of all the help he provides, still accidents and casualties are increasing. This is because we do not have the patience to follow the mentors who are the fathers. He has set them ahead of us to lead us to our places of fulfillment and achievement, but some become aggressive and lose it all.

Some of us do follow our fathers but along the way we get tired quickly. Then, instead of enduring, we look for the next exit which is an escape route and then we branch and lose our saving grace to safety, purpose and achievement. Note, however, as in the natural traffic rules, with some exits that you choose, there is no coming back. It is the same in the spirit world.

Our fathers, the escorts that God has given to us, know the road very well because they have used it over and over again and because of that they are the best experts to give us council and guidance. We cannot simply override their counsels for there is safety in them. When our escort gives us the green light to branch and go solo, they go back to bring another group of individuals who are waiting for them to bring them to safety.

Stage 7

The Furnace Fire Experience

The 7th Stage is the Furnace Fire

At this stage the vessel is now all that it will be in its shape and function, but it is not yet ready to be used. It is very brittle and any moisture or rough handling will ruin it. It must now be fired. It must go into the furnace to remove all the final traces of trapped moisture. After firing, the vessel is stronger than ever before and can now even hold water. Some vessels only go through this first firing and are found to be useful for some other purpose, for example to hold plants or to dry goods, but at this point the water will eventually seep through the small pores.

Some vessels are intended to be beautifully adorned and hold water or wine for as long as needed and they must go through a second firing. Only those specially prepared vessels are capable of withstanding the extreme furnace temperatures. First, the potter dips it into a glaze made of ground-up precious metals and earthen compounds which, oddly enough, looks like pancake batter. The vessel looks unbecoming at this stage and even ugly. The shape of the vessel can be seen but the designs and patterns are faint and are covered by a dry chalky coating. The vessel is now placed carefully into the furnace for a higher temperature firing.

Starting at room temperature, the heat of the furnace is slowly increased and carefully monitored by the potter. Over the period of about twenty hours of slowly increasing heat, the vessel begins to glow red hot. The potter watches closely through a small port to determine when the furnace starts to get close to the final temperature of about 2300 degrees Fahrenheit. At this point what was once clay from the ground changes its molecular structure and becomes like glass with all the particles fused together perfectly. If the furnace gets a little too hot, or stays at a higher temperature for too long, the vessel will collapse and melt. The master potter knows when to stop the flames in the furnace and to seal it off so that the glaze is starved of all oxygen. It is during this time, that all the vibrant colors within the glaze burst forth and fuse into the vessel. Now the exciting part happens, as each and every vessel becomes unique, even if it was dipped into the same glaze as all the others. The furnace is left to cool down on its own.

The furnace fire experience remains essential in the making of great and strong men of honor. Prior to this experience the individual will feel fresh and also feel to be in great shape and well able to function. God, however, who is the master potter, knows that we are still brittle and that some weaknesses have been trapped in some areas of our lives that he cannot overlook nor ignore for his own name's sake. The only solution, then, to those hidden weaknesses and problems is that we must be fired or must be put into the furnace fire before that moisture or that weakness trapped or hidden within us can be removed. Otherwise any rough handling which remains inevitable will ruin us and put an end to our purpose. After the Lord has put us through the fire and we have come out successfully, we will then receive the strength to handle crises and rough times which will come our way and we will also be able to offer help to other people who are going through rough times and fiery trials, like the advice of Jesus to Peter.

Depending on our purpose and assignment in life, God will make us go through the furnace fire of his choice. Some of the vessels, because of their usage and size, God allows to go through ordinary fires, but with some of the vessels that are meant to carry the oil, wine and water, their furnace fire is entirely different from that of the flower pot. Their temperatures are higher and the duration is very long. The heat is so intensive it seems not to end. Vessels of this type are meant not to fail because of the extreme temperatures they go through and survive. They are beautifully adorned and can hold oil, the wine and the water without any leakage. Only these vessels have the special grace to withstand the extreme hot temperatures.

These vessels, during the process of going through their extreme furnace fire season, look so odd and ugly, because at that stage God covers their beauty with ashes for a period, and anyone who sees them despises them like the account of Christ in the book of Isaiah.

For He grew up before Him like a tender shoot, And like a root out of parched ground; He has no stately form or majesty That we should look upon Him, Nor appearance that we should be attracted to Him. He was despised and forsaken of men, A man of sorrows and acquainted with grief; and like one from whom men hide their faces He was despised, and we did not esteem Him.
Isaiah 53:2-3

Our ministries and gifts will still be seen by all men, but at that stage what makes them attractive will be covered with pain and grief and some of our very close allies who before then pledged their allegiance will leave us and some will betray us, and even some will doubt and deny the very gift that once blessed them and made them.
God does not pick us up all of a sudden and then put us immediately into the high temperatures. He always starts it with the temperatures we are familiar with and he slowly increases it and carefully watches over us while we are being fired. As God slowly increases the fire and as our countenances begin to glow red, he draws closer to us and gives us a closer look, while we will be thinking in our hearts that he is not watching over us and that he has abandoned us and that he does not care what we are going through. He comes to us and he reminds us of his word in the book of Isaiah 43:2 that he is Jehovah SHAMMAH and he assures that we are well able and that the trials and the temptation cannot overcome us.

No temptation has overtaken you but such as is common to man; and God is faithful, who will not allow you to be tempted beyond what you are able, but with the temptation will provide the way of escape also, so that you will be able to endure it.
                    Corinthians 10:13

As in pottery, the master potter is so careful in observing the vessel in the fire and ensuring that the vessel does not sit in the fire above the specified limit of 2300 degrees Fahrenheit. He well knows that if the vessel sits in this high temperature for long it will break down and melt and cannot be made again. Folks, at the 2300 degree Fahrenheit temperature, the clay from the ground changes its molecular structure and becomes like glass. Whenever the vessel sitting in the fire gets to the point that the potter can see his image being reflected on the vessel, he starves the oxygen flaming up the fire to quench it completely. Folks, the 2300 degree Fahrenheit represents 2300 hours, which is the eleventh hour. Whenever the children of God endure patiently adversities and afflictions, at the 2300 hours which is the eleventh hour, because we have stood the test of time and did not crash nor throw in the towel, we begin to reflect the very image and the likeness of God. At that point, God rushes in for our rescue, he starves the oxygen that is flaming up the fire (the adversities) to quench them completely, because he knows that more afflictions cannot add to us nor do us any good. In fact, they would only destroy what he has spent time and resources to build for many years and it would not give him the glory. GOD WILL NOT TAKE A RISK AT THIS STAGE.

It is during and after our severest afflictions and trials that the beauty and the glory of God burst forth and fuse into us. It is then we become his handiwork of beauty and splendor. When men see us, they only see the beauty, the splendor and the glory of God; then they call us the blessed of the Lord, the vessels decked and loaded with beauty, majesty and excellence of the Almighty.

CONCLUSION

We all begin our walk with God as unworthy ugly lumps of clay that God loved and, through his only begotten son, redeemed us and brought us to his house to make us his vessels of honor and blessing. In order for us to be made for his purpose, he first placed us on his potter's wheel and he began to form us. We told God, "We have such rough edges, this is very uncomfortable, so please stop." God looked at us with his all knowing eyes and then said," My child, I have just begun; bear with me for I love you."

When he was forming us into shape with amazing curves and great designs, we said, "Lord we are in pain and we are hurting," and cried, "Please, Lord, finish with me." God looked at us with his eyes full of love and grace and said to us, "My lovely one, I am not yet done; my unfailing love is with you."

God went ahead and placed us into a cabinet with our fresh and good looks. Then we felt deprived and caged and complained bitterly that we were unloved and not involved, but God said to us, "It is my love that has kept you in this hiding place, so that the enemies will not destroy you before our time."

After the cabinet experience, it looked like we had not had enough. God proceeded to put us into the fire to remove our weaknesses and strengthen us and also to toughen us for the purpose ahead. We complained and cried, "We are dying, so please God stop these afflictions and trials; we cannot bear them any longer." God looked again at us with his ever patient and all loving eyes and said to us, "My dearly loved, I am still not done," and he whispered to us with the still small voice: *And He said to me,*

> *"My grace is sufficient for you, for power is perfected in weakness." Most gladly, therefore, I will rather boast about my weaknesses, so that the power of Christ may dwell in me.*
> 2 Corinthians 12:9

Next, God removed us from the fire and began to decorate us by painting us with priestly and royal colors that we could not see but only feel, and again we murmured and complained that we were feeling sticky and uncomfortable, and pleaded to God, "Please God, it is enough, we feel embarrassed." God amazingly looked at us once again and said to us, "My chosen ones, I am decorating you with beautiful flying colors."

Because we are vessels prepared by God himself to carry water, oil and wine which are the symbols of his nature, there was no option for him than to put us back into higher fire temperatures to seal off all pores and leaks. He left us in the fire till the 2300 hours, i.e., the eleventh hour when he could see his image and nature in us. We did not understand and did not know so we purposed in our heart to stop following him and give up on our mission, because we thought ever since we chose this way it has been affliction, trials, tribulations and test after tests. Then God drew close to us and said to us, through the fire, my grace is still sufficient for you and he recited to us:

When you pass through the waters, I will be with you; And through the rivers, they will not overflow you, When you walk through the fire, you will not be scorched, Nor will the flame burn you.
Isaiah 43:2

Then suddenly the fire went out, and the ever graceful and the ever-loving father gently stretched forth his strong and mighty hands to pick us from the oven of affliction and out came the most beautiful, most adorned, and most graceful vessel, which had been prepared before the foundations of the world, which reflects and shows forth the glory and the likeness of the Most High God, which would be highly sought by kings and priests, chief executives , presidents, prime ministers, generals and the VIPs, graceful and gifted individuals who would not fail nor perish but be life-giving vessels for God to minister life and grace to all mankind.

We would then say with tears in our eyes and our hearts full of thanksgiving and our mouth full of praise, singing songs of praise and deliverance and saying, "Our Lord, while I was an unworthy sinner, you stretched out your mighty hands to save me and made me a vessel of honor and salvation to show forth your glory and your grace to the world. To you my maker goes all the praise, adoration and thanksgiving, Amen."

We should always remember that, when trials, afflictions and persecutions come our way, they are just another spin on the potter's wheel to make us and to mold us, and not to destroy us.

> *We are afflicted in every way, but not crushed; perplexed, but not despairing; persecuted, but not forsaken; struck down, but not destroyed.*
> 2 Corinthians 4:8-9

A Sinner's Prayer

To Receive Jesus as Saviour

Dear Heavenly Father,

I come to You in the Name of Jesus.

Your Word says, "*him that cometh to me I will in no wise cast out*" (John 6:37). I know I have led a life of sin but I Know You won't cast me out, but You take me in and make me up whole again and I thank You for it.

You said in Your Word, "*Whosoever shall call upon the name of the Lord shall be saved*" (Romans 10:13). I am calling on Your name, so I know You have saved me now.

You also said "*... if thou shalt confess with thy mouth the Lord Jesus, and shalt believe in thine heart that God hath raised him from the dead, thou shalt be saved. For with the heart man believeth unto righteousness; and with mouth confession is made unto salvation*" (Romans 10:9-10). I believe in my heart Jesus Christ is the Son of God. I believe that He was raised from the dead for my justification, and I confess Him now as my Lord.

Because Your Word says, "*... with the heart man believeth unto righteousness ...*" and I do believe with my heart, I have now become the righteousness of God in Christ (2 Cor. 5:21) ... And I am saved!

Thank You, Lord!

If you have prayed this prayer, look for a Bible-believing church close to you and start attending or you can contact me with the e-mail address provided.

Bibliography

Cabajah, Joseph B. *The potter and the clay* (chap. 1). Retrieved January 10, 2010 from The Power of Truth Website http://www.cabajar.com/

Holy Ghost and Fire baptism. Reinhard Bonnke. Podcast retrieved from www.youtube.com/watch?v=3bkZWmDonpc

Laurie, Greg (1982). *The great compromise* (chap. 4). Nashville: Thomas Nelson

Moses in Egypt: retrieved January 10, 2010 from http://jasperlife.com/youth/difference/difference6-1.html

Nash, Roderick. (2001). Wilderness and the American mind. New Haven, CT: Yale University Press

Potter's Process source: http://kingdomencounter.com/articles/

Absalom pg. 114 from *Know Your Men* by Bishop Dag Heward Mills ISBN 10: 9988-596-66-9

Extraordinary Champions from Bishop Benard Jordan: www:thelawofthinking.com/

Waiting on the Lord: http://bible.org/article/waiting-lordhttp://

Potter's Wheel and Conclusion: webspace.webring.com/people/be/emeraldcity33/potter.html

About the Author

At the tender age of 12, Samuel T. Lartey had an encounter with Christ. Since then, it has been a remarkable experience with the Lord. From the age of 14, Samuel was out and about preaching at most secondary schools and hospitals in the western and central regions of Ghana, West Africa, challenging people to surrender their lives to Jesus and healing them. He is one of the founding fathers of Endtime Christian Youth Fellowship, Ghana, where they have raised pastors and many church workers and trained several missionaries with most of them still doing very well for the Lord.

Currently a Senior Associate Minister at Lawrence Tetteh's Worldwide Miracle Outreach Church International, London, United Kingdom, and a member of Morris Cerullo GVA UK, he is a sought after revivalist and conference speaker. Having had a physical visitation of Christ twice, Samuel is so blessed with the ministry of prophetic preaching, working of miracles and as a teacher of the Word. He is a minister's minister and carries a strong message to the church.

Samuel graduated with a Bachelor of Business Administration degree and furthered it with a post-graduate advanced diploma in Computer Science in UK and Master of Science in Refugee Studies at The London Southbank University.

Samuel resides in London, UK, with his wife Maud and their twin daughters, Jerielle and Joelle. You may contact him for speaking appointments, ministers' and leadership seminars, and his CDs, books and for other enquiries at:
concord82@yahoo.com

The Finished Work of the Carpenter

Show me your hand Lord when selfishly I pray;
Show me your hand Lord when I want my own way.
Show me your hand Lord lest I forget,
That it was my life not yours you died to perfect.

Poetry and Artprint by Gabriel H. Vaughn ©2010 Used by permission